Michal Fisher

Finding Your Career Path without Losing Your Mind

Emotional Management for Job-Seekers and Career-Changers

Michal Fisher

Finding Your Career Path without Losing Your Mind

Emotional Management
for Job-Seekers and Career-Changers

Copyright © 2013
by Michal Fisher

https://www.facebook.com/FisherMichal

Language editing: Anne Christiansen
Cover and interior design: Rachel Weiss

Free special bonus -
10 Hot Tips to Finding Your Career Path without Losing Your Mind:

http://activepage.co.il/TenHotTips

Contents

Introduction

Congratulations!

If you're reading this book, you're probably building a new business, looking for a new job or striving to otherwise fulfill yourself professionally. In any case, you deserve congratulations as you are facing one of the most exciting phases of your life. Nowadays so many people succumb to unfulfilling jobs; according to a survey conducted by the company Right Management and published in Forbes Magazine in August 2012, only 19% of employees in the United States and Canada say they are satisfied with their jobs. The decision to make a change and build the career you desire takes courage, determination and faith. Kudos for that!

As a life-coach and a career-development group facilitator I have accompanied dozens of people on their journeys towards the career of their dreams. Over and over again I have witnessed the process of people fulfilling old dreams; people who are looking for the best way to bring themselves to the fore, and to express their abilities and talents; people who desire to make a contribution, and to share with others what most excites and moves them. They find a way to build a financially and emotionally rewarding career.

But ... it is not always easy.

Career-change reaches deep down inside us, touching issues of self-esteem, self-image, identity, values and meaning. Along with a burning desire to contribute, make a change and develop yourself, you indisputably encounter fears, concerns, anxieties and self-doubt. Perhaps you have experienced disappointments, failures and rejections from clients or potential employers. You may have faced criticism and doubt from friends or family, or have felt loss or guilt over choices you made or did not make.

That is why this book was conceived. It does not matter which goal you're pursuing, whether it be building a new business or looking for a new job. This guide is designed to help you, step by step, to build up your confidence, raise your energy level, boost your motivation, and give you tools to deal with setbacks, doubts, criticism and guilt.

I do hope that you, like my clients, find that building a new career can be an exciting and empowering process; that you find yourself getting up in the morning with a big smile on your face, that you enjoy the journey and grow as a person. Enthusiasm and positive energy will help you achieve your purpose – building the career you really desire – easily and happily.

My story

I also went through a significant and challenging process constructing the career I today recognize as my calling. When I was a child I dreamed of helping people to grow and to realize their potential, while also aspiring to become a writer. I wrote my first book, about the adventures of Rosa, in sixth grade. Every year I was elected to the class's social committee. I organized social events and edited classroom and school newspapers.

My academic beginnings were likewise promising; I was an honors student and skipped two grades. However, once school was over and "real life" began, something got lost. My scholastic abilities did not help me when there were no exams and transcripts, and no one from the outside who could define the right thing for me to do. The family circle and social environment I grew up in had taught me to pursue "safe" and "stable" directions. Words like passion, pleasure and livelihood couldn't coexist in my world. My desire to create, to be independent and pave my unique way seemed like a distant dream or a fantasy fairy tale. I earned a B.A. in psychology, but for many years found myself employed in administrative, marketing and customer service positions, which are great lines of work, but not for me.

The significant change occurred in my early 30s. I was unemployed, felt stuck and did not know where to go from there. I had already realized that the values I was raised with did not work for me, but I could not identify an alternative path. However, life, in its mysterious and wonderful ways, showed me how moments of emptiness and vagueness can become moments of revelation and provide answers. For the first time in my life I came across the realms of meditation and guided imagery, which have since become a way of living – comprising listening, acceptance, observation, and many moments of joy. I also stumbled, purely by coincidence, upon a training course for group facilitators offered by the unemployment office. At the end of the course I was offered the opportunity to lead a fascinating career-development group of single mothers who hadn't worked for at least the past five years (some of them had never worked). Running a group filled me with passion, satisfaction and meaning. The North Star of my calling started to shine for me .I enrolled in a Master's degree program in group leadership through the arts. I started my own business and began to write again. The book you're now reading is my second endeavor since the days of Rosa.

Along the way I had to deal with a lack of trust in my abilities from my immediate surroundings, including my family, and I experienced quite a few doubts, failures, painful feelings and disappointments. I learned to trust my inner voice, listen well to my dreams, grow from my fears and insist on what really matters to me. I share here with you in this book what I learned in this process. You will read inspiring stories of my own experiences, episodes of my clients (all names and identifying details have been disguised), and stories and quotes from successful people.

I will also share with you the insights I've acquired in the worlds of business training, psychology and various spiritual teachings, especially Buddhism and the world of meditation, which is now part of my everyday life. Also, because it's important to me that you get the most out of this manual, it includes tips, tools and practical exercises that you can implement today to find your own way to your dream career, all the while maintaining a high level of energy, motivation, passion, optimism and joy.

How to make the most of this book?

This is a great question, one to which you alone best know the answer.
The following questions will help you focus on what matters most to you, and help you commit yourself to making the most of this book.

What do you want to get out of this book?
(For example, learning how to deal with my fears, raising my motivation to look for a new job, believing more in myself and in my service's/product's value.)

_____

_____

What are your own key guidelines to maximizing the value of this book?
(For example, to open myself up to new knowledge, or to apply the knowledge I acquire.)

_____

_____

The book is divided into eight chapters presenting the chief emotions and feelings inherent in the career-building process: Love & Freedom, Happiness, Self-Esteem, Fear & Anxiety, Failure & Disappointment, Anger, Grief & Loss, and Guilt. In each chapter you'll come upon information, tools, tips, inspiring stories and practical exercises to foster positive emotions and to deal with difficult ones.

This guide takes a holistic approach, so each chapter complements the others. Therefore, I recommend that you read the chapters in full. The order in which you read the chapters does not matter. In one chapter you will read that determination and perseverance in light of failure are keys to success, while another chapter reads that it's important to let go and not hold onto goals at all costs. "To everything there is a season, and a time for every purpose under the heaven," said King Solomon, the wisest of men. Each moment is different, so what is right for you today won't necessarily be right for you tomorrow.

Find the right way for you to read this book and apply its contents. Some people read manuals sequentially from beginning to end. Others prefer to read about their own most burning topic at any given time. Some people apply all the exercises, and others draw inspiration and exercise more selectively.

What is your style?

My advice is that in whatever you choose to do, it is important to persevere. This book offers many exercises, some of which are designed for one-time application and some for use over a period of time. You should begin to notice a change in about three weeks, if you practice daily. Changing habits and implementing new ways of thinking is like yoga for the brain – this takes time and systematic work. Therefore, it's better to practice 15 minutes every day than an hour and a half once a week. The information and inspiration you draw from this book represent only the first step. Application, determination, perseverance, courage and commitment to yourself are your key to occupational self-realization.

Another hot tip is to keep an **"emotions journal"** in which you freely write down what you feel. Writing your feelings in a journal will help you avoid any accumulation of anger, frustration and pain, and help you find creative solutions to bothersome issues. This book also offers writing exercises for your emotions journal.

In conclusion: this guide is about dealing with feelings while changing career or building a new one. But first and foremost it is a book about love, relationships and growth. In other words, it is a book about life. Managing a successful career is not a recipe for baked potatoes. A successful career is an act of love, passion, and finding meaning. It is a privilege to live a life of love, to arise each morning to a day full of meaning; and the way to this end passes through the tapestry of your values, your dreams, and your old pains and fears.

I hope this guide in front of you will be a loyal friend on your journey, and will help you look deep inside, dig up hidden treasures within yourself, and emerge stronger, clearer, more peaceful, more successful, and, even – happier.

Shall we start?

Fear & Anxiety

The price of fear on your career

On your path of building your career, it's natural that all kinds of emotions arise. Some are welcome and positive such as excitement, enthusiasm or joy, and some are a little less pleasant. Anxiety and fear are definitely in the second group.

Anxiety can be paralyzing, depressing and ... scary. It's only natural that people often try to avoid feelings of fear and so "bypass" them in different ways:

Repression: Sometimes the way people deal with anxiety is by suppressing it, and not letting it undermine their actions. I once asked my brother, who used to be an army officer, how he had dealt with his fears on the battlefield. He said: "I did not feel anything. The will to survive and to live through the battle required so many resources that there was no room for feelings like pain or fear." But those feelings do not go away. They emerge later, at home, in civilian life.

The professional world can also feel like a battlefield, as if it's a war of survival where the strongest wins, and there is not much room for emotions. The price, though, will probably be paid in one's personal life: the man or woman who learned to be tough and to repress their emotions might feel aversion towards pain and weakness and have difficulties maintaining close relationships.

Escape: Another coping strategy is to avoid facing fear. That is, to avoid challenging or stressful situations by pretending that everything is fine, even if it's not. Examples of such an escape can be neglect of accumulating debts and pretending that the financial situation is under control, or refraining from taking active, initiative steps to promote the business.

You must be aware of the heavy price you pay by surrendering to fears. You've probably seen how procrastination in the face of your problems makes them bigger, more complicated and more costly. You are probably aware of all those useful things that you refrain from doing, all those creative and original things you would do if you dared. It reminds me of a sentence I once heard: "All you want is on the other side of fear."

What is on the other side of your fear?

One of the most important things in dealing with anxieties and fears is what is known as "stepping out of the comfort zone," meaning: changing habits of escape and suppression that reduce and limit us, preventing us from being the creative, full-of-life, vigorous and energetic human beings we have the potential to be. Yielding to fears means giving up the right to live your life to the fullest.

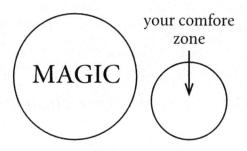

A DRAWING EXERCISE:
Befriending anxiety

Find some quiet moments for yourself and answer the following question:
What would I do today/this week/this year if I were not afraid?
Make a list of at least three things you would do if fear were not stopping you.
Choose one thing from the list to do this week.

EXERCISE:
Clearing out feelings of fear

If you feel stuck, worried or restless, it might be because you are afraid. Maybe someone told you something that undermined your confidence; perhaps you received a negative response from a position you applied for, or maybe you were rejected or criticized in your personal life.
As with other negative feelings – anger, guilt or pain – it is important to express what you feel in order to "clear out" the emotion and move on.

Take a few quiet minutes, ten or fifteen will suffice, and write about your fears and concerns. Don't be rational about it; don't analyze yourself or the situation (You can do this later.) Just be as true and genuine to yourself as you can, and allow all your emotions to emerge. Obviously, fear and anxiety are often accompanied by anger and pain. Let it all out. As you follow the trail of your emotions you might gain some interesting insights.

Writing may enable you to put things in perspective and help you move on, or help you realize that there is a real problem that requires your attention. Continue to write over the next few days until you feel lighter and calmer, and have a clearer picture about how to deal with what is bothering you.

Anxiety and career-change

Sometimes what holds us back is larger than a specific fear like initiating a meeting or being interviewed for a new job. When we make a significant change in life – and embarking on a new career is definitely such a change – one might be overwhelmed by **anxiety**.

You may be beset by anxiety when you go on interviews and repeatedly receive rejections; you are afraid you might not find a good job before you consume all your savings. Anxiety might result after a launch evening to which only your family and a few friends showed up. Or anxiety might strike for no apparent reason at all. You are constantly worried. You sleep poorly, feel restless, and begin to think that all this talk about a life of purpose and fulfillment of one's dreams is for the pampered and rich, but not for you – an ordinary person – who is just trying to make ends meet.

Anxiety can manifest itself in thoughts like: "My business will fail," "I'll never develop enough customers," "I have no chance of succeeding in job interviews," "I'll always stay poor and unemployed," and so on. One of the most disturbing symptoms of anxiety is the feeling of helplessness; paralysis in the face of a challenge that seems just too big to handle. In addition, anxiety may be accompanied by physiological and psychological symptoms such as palpitations, chest pain, migraines, stomach irritation, sweating, poor sleep, shortness of breath, emotional distress, a choking sensation, incessant worries, confusion and more.

Anxiety is a deep-seated fear that things will crash, collapse or spin out of control. It is an inner conviction that if things do not work out properly you will fall into an abyss. Often it comes with a strong feeling of foreboding, of impending doom, that something horrible is about to happen. If you suffer from anxiety I'm sure you know very well what I'm talking about.

When I decided to make a career change and pursue my dream of becoming a group counselor and life coach, I encountered a wide range of emotions. Anxiety was certainly one of the dominant ones. Most of my life I'd worked in jobs I didn't really like that much, but I believed it was the way to make a living. I learned at home that work is a serious matter, and making dreams come true is a luxury activity for leisure time. I had an excellent teacher in this regard: my father. My beloved father had forgone his dream to engage in teaching Torah (that is, Jewish and rabbinic scholarship) and chose instead to work as a computer programmer so as to provide for our large family. However, he didn't relinquish his dream altogether, and devoted his afternoons and Saturdays to Torah study and teaching congregation members. The message I received was that there was a time and place for work, and one for hobbies, but they didn't go together. Work should be undertaken safely and responsibly.

Becoming a doctor or a bank employee, for example, certainly met these criteria. But I just wasn't inclined this way. My heart pulled me in directions that were obviously not serious enough, such as writing and creative work. Moreover, my dream of starting my own business as a freelancer was classified under the category of "extremely dangerous" because being self-employed was considered a massively irresponsible gamble.

In retrospect, I'm not surprised that I felt panicked in the first weeks after leaving my job. Although I felt tremendous joy and excitement about setting off on a new path, I also suffered from tension and restlessness, I slept poorly and had difficulties concentrating. I was overwhelmed by worries and self-doubt: "How will I manage?" I wondered. The question "What have I done!?" gnawed at me.

The truth is that anxiety is more connected to our past than to our future.

Unlike the natural fear aroused by an imminent and tangible threat (a snarling dog chasing you down the street), anxiety is a sense of danger that stems from messages we picked up from (mostly) childhood experiences. The psychologist Donald Winnicott proposed that it "... turns out to be very simple. I contend that clinical fear of breakdown is the fear of a breakdown that has already been experienced." This is the most accurate definition of anxiety that I know of; being afraid of a hypothetical future danger – usually imagined and irrational – that has already threatened us in the past. The threatening event happened when we were too young to process it or adequately cope with it. It became a dark, lurking inner shadow. Now, past is projected onto future as anxiety. An example of this is Maya's story, presented in one of the next passages.

The good news is that anxiety is a normal and natural emotion. And even better news is that anxiety (and its best friend, guilt) is often an indication that you are on the right track. If you were not breaking through the boundaries of the known and familiar, the warning bells wouldn't be ringing. If they ring, let them – and give yourself credit for your courage to make a change.

Three steps for dealing with anxiety

Here are the steps for dealing with anxiety:

Breathe: Anxiety and fear often shorten the breath. Remind yourself from time to time to take some deep breaths, and prolong the **exhaling** above and beyond the usual rhythm.

Make friends with fear: You can treat fear and anxiety as unpleasant or intimidating emotions, but you do not have to. Professor Mario Livio, a senior researcher at the Hubble Space Telescope, and author of *The Golden Ratio* and *Is God a Mathematician*? says that the way to deal with fear is to be curious about it. In his own words: "The cure for fear is curiosity." Often, when I think of something I would like to do and yet I'm scared of, I intentionally approach the fear rather than following my natural instinct to stay clear of it. I remind myself that I may be curious about what would happen if I dare do that thing that scares me. It turns the fear into a game.

If the notions behind "making friends with fear" sound far-fetched to you, at the very least you need to familiarize yourself with your anxieties and agree to look them in the eye. You can't deal with that which you're avoiding contact with and running from.

Dare: Step out of the comfort zone of your familiar behavioral patterns. Identifying and understanding your anxieties and escape mechanisms is necessary but not enough. It is imperative to deal with situations that frighten you. Dare to do what you love; express your desires and emotions; be assertive; allow yourself to be acknowledged for your achievements. Challenge yourself. Allow yourself to succeed and recognize that you can enjoy it. Cherish small successes. Say good words to yourself – that you deserve to be happy, successful and to be heard. Encourage and forgive yourself if you stumble or make mistakes along the way. Create a supportive environment, and connect with people who support your growth.

This last point – Dare – is so important that I will elaborate on it separately later.

Observation meditation: "Being with" anxiety

Anxiety is just an emotion. If you treat it like a little kid who wants your attention it will be much easier for you to address. It won't disappear if you run away from it.

Dealing with unpleasant feelings is not necessarily done by "fixing" them, but rather by "being with" them. Observing your anxiety (or anger and pain for that matter) – and the physical sensations, emotions and thoughts that accompany it – can make all the difference. Great relief results from just allowing yourself to "be with" what you feel at the moment and not rushing to resolve it right away.

Being cheerful and smiley-faced is so highly valued in our society (take a look at your friends' Facebook timeline photos for instance), that sometimes it turns into a cumbersome chore. In his interesting essay "History of Emotions," Professor Peter Stearns depicts how the U.S. and Western Europe have dealt with the "threat of emotions" by embracing cheerfulness as the predominantly appropriate emotion as early as the eighteenth century:

> *Once launched, the new insistence on cheerfulness gained ground steadily. By the late twentieth century it affected labor relations as well as commercial interactions, with workers expected to display a sunny disposition as proof of their employability.*

Well, that can be so exhausting! Sometimes all we need is support, a shoulder to lean on and someone to hold us. For yourself, be that person who holds you. The concept behind observation meditation is "being with" things on an intimate level. You will see that feelings come and go, and often, when the drama is gone, the feelings subside as well.

Try to "be with" your emotions using the following observation meditation:

Sit in a quiet place where there will be no interruptions. Turn off the phone. Set an alarm clock for 10-20 minutes. Close your eyes and assume a comfortable posture that allows you to sit with your back straight but not stiff.

Pay attention to the natural movement of the breathing, to the incoming and outgoing air. Focus on the area where the breathing sensation is most dominant – it could be your abdomen, your chest or the nostril area. After a few natural breaths, shift your focus of attention to the sensations of anxiety in your body. Do you feel a knot in your stomach? Contraction in your throat? Does it affect your breathing? Making it faster? Shallower?

Observe these feelings as an onlooker or witness. Don't interpret the flow of your emotions or try to understand them. If you feel anxiety taking over, it's

OK. Keep on breathing. One of my meditation teachers once said to me that even if you are emotionally overwhelmed 90% of the time, and objectively observing only 10% of it, the meditation is still effective enough.

Approach your anxiety with curiosity and treat yourself with affection and caring. That's really what matters.

A DRAWING EXERCISE:
Befriending anxiety

Set aside 10-20 quiet minutes.

Get a sheet of plain paper and crayons. Make a drawing of your fear. Let the feeling of fear take form. Your drawing may be concrete (e.g., a monster or an animal) or abstract.
Look at the drawing. Does fear arise in you? Good.

Display the drawing in a place where you can see it frequently. Look at it every day with the intention of making friends with your fear. After a week of two, throw it away.

EXERCISE:
Taking action; small steps of courage

Let's examine your more specific fears, those which stop you from taking those small steps that can promote your career. For example, is there anyone who can possibly help you but you're afraid to make the call, so you continue to procrastinate? Are you afraid of giving a presentation at your neighborhood's community center even though you want people to know about you and your services? Do you balk at talking to the bank manager or tax authorities? Do you have an unresolved issue with an employee/client/colleague but avoid discussing it with them?

Make a list of those small actions you set to the side again and again.
Look at the list. Is there one thing you can do today? Or in the coming week?

In my experience, if you adopt an attitude of curiosity, like of "Hmmm ... I wonder what would happen if I do this?" it is easier to find the courage to take that step.

Now let's look together more deeply into our anxieties: at how they developed and at how they run our lives. Let's look into the eyes of fear. This will help us control it.

What is the source of anxiety?

Many of us learned in childhood that success and self-expression are dangerous, and despite the strong desire to achieve and to engage in meaningful activity, we harbor anxiety that success will demand a high price.

Sometimes anxiety overcomes us to the point that it blocks our career progress. An example of this is Maya, a woman in her thirties who participated in a career-change workshop. Maya worked for years in a technical job that didn't suit her creative talents. The hours were long and the pay was low. Maya stood out as a diligent, professional and responsible employee, but she felt exploited and even victimized. Every morning for years she got up at 7 am, went to work and hated every minute of it. Maya knew she wanted a change, but she did not know which change and how to make it. When she came home at the end of a workday she was too tired to think about new options.

Maya shared with the group that as a young girl she was required to take care of her little brother and be responsible for the household. Her parents were poor immigrants who each worked two jobs and were rarely at home. She received a subtle message that being a kid, playing and frolicking, was selfish, irresponsible and even dangerous. (Once while she played in her room her brother accidentally poured boiling water on himself in the kitchen. Her parents were furious.) Maya had to grow up fast, set aside her desires and take responsibility at home.

Choosing a tedious and unrewarding workplace was an unconscious natural continuation of what Maya had learned and been accustomed to as a child. She chose an arduous job that didn't reflect her desires and talents, just as she had had to assume the burden of taking care of her brother and set aside her own wishes. However, this job also served as a sort of addiction, and it played an important role in Maya's life: the whole time she worked there she avoided the looming feelings of anxiety that struck her when she began to think seriously about pursuing her desires and realizing her potential. This job was part of Maya's psychological defense mechanism. It had helped her escape the deep anger she felt towards her parents and the anxiety and guilt called by her attempts to find her unique voice and realize her dreams.

During the workshop, Maya slowly acknowledged the rage that she harbored towards her parents, which she had suppressed all these years due to shame and guilt. "How can I be angry at parents who worked so hard to provide for us?" she cried. At the same time a new desire was emerging within her – a dream to open a bakery and put into practice her love of baking. The first steps of building her own business and relinquishing the familiar behavioral pattern (sacrificing her own desires for the sake of others) were accompanied by fears, self-doubt and worries. Maya discovered she was afraid that if she were true to herself, people would reject her, in accordance with the underlying message of conditional love she received from her parents: "To get us to love you, be responsible and mature and put the rest of your nonsense aside."

Maya finally realized that the difficulty she had in leaving her drab, unsatisfactory job was partly due to it having been a shelter from her anxiety and self-doubt. "Confronting all these doubts, anxieties and feelings of loneliness is sometimes so discouraging," she remarked wistfully. However, despite the difficulty, Maya found inner courage and the strength to look inward, and move to the other side of her fear with increasing creativity, joy and self-confidence.

Maya's story is a classic example of an experience common to many people, as shown in the following diagram:

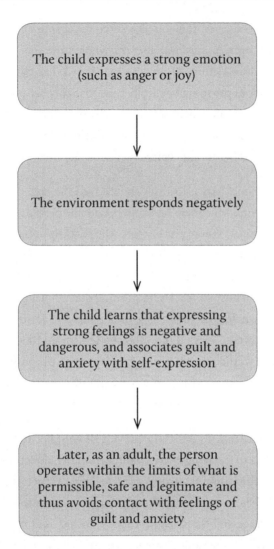

The Triangle of Conflict

The Triangle of Conflict, developed by the psychoanalyst David Malan is a simple graphic illustration of the formation of anxiety and how to alleviate it.

This simple triangle can help you gain deep insights about yourself.

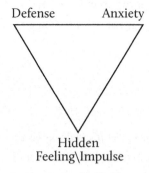

Defense   Anxiety

Hidden
Feeling\Impulse

According to the Triangle of Conflict, underlying every defense mechanism is anxiety that is related to an impulse or a strong emotion that was blocked during childhood. Defenses are all those negative behavior patterns with which people hurt themselves, such as addictions, fear of crowds, victimization, a tendency to please others, obsessive compulsive disorder (OCD), depression, exam anxiety and fear of intimacy.

Defenses are ways in which we avoid expressing that which was not legitimate in childhood – whether it was anger or pain, or conversely, a sense of joy and playfulness. Dismantling destructive behavior patterns (i.e. defenses) often entails dealing with the underlying anxiety, guilt and anger. This is why people who undergo psychotherapy are often surprised that the way to happiness is not always pleasant; because traveling the path to self-expression awakens old pain, regret about missed opportunities, fear and other dormant emotions.

Malan's model suggests that stepping out from the safe haven of our familiar behavior patterns, especially if they are self-destructive, inevitably gives rise to anxiety because those patterns were developed to ensure psychological survival in childhood. Hence, we can expect some warning lights to turn on in our heads if we dare to deviate from our safe route, from what is known and familiar.

You surely understand what that means: **anxiety and self-doubt are natural responses to a change in situation.** And more importantly – anxiety is an indication that you are on the right path. You are growing and beginning to really touch all that you suppressed in the past, something which is now crying out for expression and fulfillment. It's your time to start living for real.

WRITING EXERCISE:
Letting the demons out

To overcome fears and anxieties it's really important to have a clear picture of what truly scares you, to be curious about your fears.

What are your deepest fears regarding your career? Are you afraid to fail? Afraid of being unemployed and impoverished? Are you afraid of the reactions of your family, friends, colleagues and peers if you really do make it? Do people around you think you are taking too big a risk and recommend that you go safe and avoid trying new things? Or maybe you are afraid of success? Afraid of accepting responsibility? Are you afraid of rejection? Afraid that you will give it all and yet others will think you're not good enough?

Find a few quiet minutes to yourself. Make a list of everything that makes you frightened or anxious. Elaborate and be as specific as possible. Let all the demons run free. Do not hold anything back:

For example:

Fear of failure: *"I'm afraid to fail, it seems like the end of the world to me." "It's my last chance. If I fail, I could never try again. People will feel sorry for me and I will get stuck in a boring job for the rest of my life." "I'm afraid to fail and to find out that I am not as talented as I thought."*

Fear of success: *"I'm afraid to succeed because that means being alone and lonely." "People won't like me because of what I am, but will only want to use me." "All successful people walked over cold corpses on their way to the top. I do not want to be this kind of person."*

Other common fears and anxieties:

Fear of loss: *a fear that success comes with a price tag and that downfall is inevitable ("It's too good to be true. There must be a 'catch'.")*

Fear of loneliness: *stems from a belief that successful people have no true friends.*

Fear of losing quality time with family: *especially typical of women, who fear that their career will prosper at the expense of their family.*

Fear of relinquishing freedom: a perception that committing to a profession means boredom, lack of diversification and loss of spontaneity.

Fear of exploitation: similar to fear of loneliness, it's a conviction that others associate with successful people only to take advantage of their money, their connections and so on.

Fear of liability: a belief that success – especially if a person becomes a public or recognized figure – entails turning into someone else, more "respectable" and representational, and that one will lose their right to be human and flawed.

Fear of dying: a belief that if you live to your full potential you will cease to exist.

Relearn that it's safe to express yourself

According to Malan, in order to fully express yourself, you must sever the link between anxiety/guilt/fear and the emotion you originally suppressed. That is, learning that it is safe to be emotionally authentic, to feel anger or joy, to desire, to create and play. Then the destructive behavior pattern (the defense mechanism) will dissipate.

Take for example the fear of confrontation: it is a very common fear that undermines one's ability to stand up for their rights and freely express their desires. Did your childhood environment encourage or discourage assertive behavior?

If your anger distressed or upset your parents (when you were angry they said: "Look how you made Mom cry!"; "Anger is forbidden! Behave yourself!"), then you may have developed feelings of guilt and anxiety regarding anger ("I hurt my mom and dad," "I'm bad when I'm angry."). You learned to repress your anger and you might have even lost contact with it. In adults, potentially contentious situations evoke anxiety and feelings of guilt, making it difficult to display assertive and firm behavior, and to stand up for your rights and promote your wishes. Perhaps you do not even know what you want, because anger is, in essence, a positive motivational force to make a change, and express and fulfill oneself. The anxiety and guilt you've learned to associate with anger made you prone to pleasing others. Perhaps you also suffer from psychosomatic symptoms such as migraines and digestive problems.

Practicing assertive expression will break the connection between anger and anxiety; you will see that assertive and emotionally honest behavior will help you pursue your goals, make you feel better about yourself, and result in more appreciation from the people around you. The more you practice expressing your will and desires, dare to express your opinions even when the other side thinks otherwise, and tell people if something bothers you or hurts you, the sooner will the fear of conflict diminish and the need to please others drop significantly.

EXERCISE:
Committing to success

1. *Look at the list of your biggest fears which you indentified in the previous exercise. Create the inverse of your fears by turning them into positive statements about yourself. For example, instead of "Successful people step on others on their way up," write: "Success makes me a better person." Instead of "Committing to a job will take away my freedom," write: "Committing to a job will set me free."*

2. *Contemplate each positive statement: What does it mean to you? How can you make it happen? Make new commitments to yourself, and specify the actions you will do to stick to your commitment.*

For example:

Think of what being a better person means to you. For instance, you could commit to acting honestly and fairly with all customers and employees.
Think about what makes you feel free. If it's about time management you could write: "I commit to balancing work and leisure; I will go out with friends at least once a week," and so on.

Be specific. *If your idea of freedom is about being your own boss you might decide to open your own business or search for a job with a high level of responsibility and authority.*

Dare

" *A monk once asked the Buddha:*
"What to do with fear?"
The Buddha replied:
"It depends on what you are doing at the moment;
if you are sitting – sit down with the fear;
if you're standing – stand with the fear;
and if you walking –
keep on walking with the fear." "

Do you look your fears in the eye and step out of your comfort zone? Do you dare and take risks? If so, well done. Stepping out of your comfort zone is vitally important. The Triangle of Conflict illustrates how our safe zone and behavioral patterns are often no less than an emotional prison. You have probably realized by now that fear is an inseparable part of your progress, and I hope this helps keep you going even in the presence of fear. This is a huge step on the way to success. The noteworthy English singer Chris Martin once said that he often suffers from bad dreams about concerts going bad. But it does not stop him from getting up on stage again. In the spirit of the Buddha above, the psychologist Dr. Tal Ben-Shahar writes in his book *Happier*: "To bring about change in our lives we need courage. **And courage does not mean not being afraid, but rather being afraid and still carrying forward.**" [Emphasis in the original.] Rumi, the Sufi poet who lived in the thirteenth century, went even further, saying: "Run from what's comfortable. Forget safety. Live where you fear to live. Destroy your reputation. Be notorious."

As mentioned, it is a mistake to wait for fear to fade before taking action, because this is an ideal way to ensure that nothing will happen soon, if ever. Fear triggers escape or freeze mechanisms, and sometimes the best strategy is to make precisely the opposite move – to confront that which scares us, to be proactive, to look in the eyes of the monster. **Usually, just taking the action, no matter the consequences, will give you a feeling of tremendous achievement.** Often the best way to dispel fear is to undertake exactly what you are afraid of.

I remember the first time I led a workshop, at the end of the group facilitators' training course in which I participated. Unfortunately for me, leading a workshop was a requirement of the qualification process. I would have gladly relinquished it, because I suffered from public-speaking anxiety. I was to deliver a short workshop to the other students with whom I had studied intensively and spent the past three months. But at the moment of truth, as fear gripped my throat, I could not remember their names. I was afraid to the extent that parts of my brain shut down. Somehow I managed to conduct the workshop – without once calling my friends by name.

This was my first experience in group-facilitating, but several years have passed since then. Gradually, thanks to recurrent experience in giving lectures and delivering workshops, I have reached a point where my anxiety has subsided and I actually enjoy working with groups and usually feel relaxed and calm (although always excited). One of the highlights affirming my triumph at the end of a long difficult road was at the conclusion of a weekend meditation seminar – when I went on stage before an audience of 150 participants and related my experiences as a kitchen volunteer during the seminar. I shared the fact that I chose to volunteer in the kitchen even though I had no idea how to cook or prepare food. "Volunteering in the kitchen was a daily challenge," I said. Everyone laughed when I shared that: "For me, today, being in charge of dressing a salad is much more frightening than speaking in front of 150 people."

Well, in this life there's always room to grow.

Perfectionism and anxiety

Do you need to do everything perfectly? Are you waiting to be one hundred percent ready before applying for a job? Are you constantly improving your website and putting off going live with it?

Perfectionism is another manifestation of anxiety. It stems from the fear of making mistakes, to be rejected or to fail.

Ofer Melamed, a former marketing vice president of a large high-tech company and now a business coach, once said to me: "We change and learn all the time." He coaches people to achieve business success by focusing on dealing with procrastination and perfectionism.

"Whatever you do, tomorrow you can do differently, better," he went on.

"I told you so!" cried the little perfectionist in me.

"But," he continued, "It's also comforting."

Hmmm ... I raised an internal eyebrow.

"It means that whatever you do, it will always be imperfect, so you better do it today. There is no reason to wait."

"Okay ..." I mumbled uncertainly.

To illustrate his point, Ofer showed me his business card: "This is my seventh version, and I'm sure I'll change it again in the future."

"Life is imperfect" is one of the principles you learn through meditation practice. No matter how important you are in your own eyes, how many degrees you have acquired, or how many people follow you on Twitter, you are still flooded with petty and boring thoughts once you've decided to focus on breathing: thoughts about your bank balance, the supermarket shopping list, calorie calculations from lunch and anger at the driver who cut you off this morning on your way to work. All these (and more) take over your mind until you remember to direct your attention back to breathing, and it won't be long before you get distracted again. Futile attempts to become the "perfect meditator" remind you again and again that there is no such thing. The only thing you can do is try the best you can right now.

There is a story about a young novice who joined a monastery and asked one of the older monks: "When your mind wanders during meditation practice (he already knew that the mind constantly drifts) what do you think of?"

"About sex" replied the older monk.

An hour of meditation is one amusing reminder of our humanity and lack of perfection.

Recognizing that we are not perfect is really liberating. It gives us permission to be light, playful and daring. Accepting our imperfection also relaxes the fear of making mistakes. Mistakes will always happen, so at least enjoy it when you make them.

OBSERVATION EXERCISE:
What would I do if I needn't do it perfectly?

Take a sheet of paper and write this title at the top of the page:
What would I do this day/week/month if I didn't need to do it perfectly?

Write down all the answers that come to mind, even the most outlandish. When you're done, go through the list and choose three tasks to accomplish during the coming day, week or month.

I recommend doing this exercise once a week, especially if you are a perfectionist.

Fear and anxiety –
more tips and ideas to think about

About regret: Studies show that people usually regret things they have not done, and not the things they have done. How does this relate to you?

Think about the worst-case scenario: Sometimes it helps to think about the worst that can happen: What if I fail? What if I'm rejected? What if I don't get that job? What's the worst that could happen? Usually you'll see that whatever the answer is, it's not that bad. Or, it's a price worth paying.

Choosing a worthwhile goal: One of the best criteria by which to choose a worthwhile goal is that it should excite and also **scare** you. Goals that do not frighten you at all, that hold no risk whatsoever, are goals that won't help you grow beyond your limits and get to a place where dreams come true. Do that which accelerates your heartbeat.

Preparation and information gathering: These are anchors that can give you a sense of security. If you repeatedly put off making a decision, one of the tools that can help you move forward is researching the issue you are dealing with. Knowledge is power. For example, if you are undecided about a particular job, gather information on the company, the terms of employment, the nature of the job. Before an important meeting gather intel on the client, the employer or your target audience. Ask questions like: What interests them? What is important to them? What bothers them? Then formulate in advance the most significant points that you want to discuss or emphasize.

One small reservation about preparation and information gathering: If you constantly postpone a meeting, interview or venture "to prepare for it," ask yourself, in all honesty, whether you are really busy with necessary preparation, or inhibited by fear. There comes a point when you must take the plunge!

Processing fear: Another anchor to help you deal with fear is processing it through talking or writing. This is another way of looking the monster in the eye. Write down or talk to someone about what scares you, really look into it, and ask yourself questions such as: Why does it scare me so much? What is it about this situation or person that shakes me up? Looking into yourself takes a lot of courage. Sometimes the answers may feel embarrassing: "I'm scared of him because I really want him to love me," "I'm afraid of her because she reminds me of my mother." Remember that many times fear is an expression of that little child inside of you.

Processing your fears will help you overcome them. Just take care to actually **do** something about them and to avoid getting stuck in the processing phase.

Fear and anxiety are "cold" emotions: When people say that a fearful situation sends "chills up their spine," it's quite an accurate depiction of what fear triggers. Sometimes it's helpful to warm yourself up emotionally. Warm feelings are love (at one pole) or anger (at the other pole). When you are fearful it might be advisable to be with someone you love, do something you like doing, or watch a good-spirited movie. Soon I will suggest a way to harness anger for the purpose of allaying anxiety.

Avoid procrastination: Procrastination is a tendency to put off doing something, especially boring, unpleasant or intimidating tasks. An excellent habit is to do your most unpleasant tasks in the morning. It will take a weight off your chest and free up your day for the more enjoyable stuff.

Make decisions quickly: This is one of the characteristics of successful people.

Think about the added value you give: This is a great approach to bring to meetings, lectures or presentations. Instead of thinking about how to prove yourself and impress other people, think about what you're going to give to those people you are about to meet. When you think in terms of giving, you connect to your added value and to your strengths. Instead of waiting for approval, you will receive it naturally. In addition, such thinking connects you to love, and this is a fantastic energy to bring to any human encounter. Value you give can be humor, respect, appreciation, knowledge, inspiration or any other qualities that characterize you.

Self-talk: It is also a good method for dealing with fear. Often, I encourage myself all the way to the phone, to an interview, to a lecture, to a meeting: "You can do it, you've got it what it takes, you have so much to give." I remind myself of the value I bring, and give myself permission to make mistakes, play and enjoy. Brainwashing is a terrific tool.

Determined action raises self-confidence: Moving forward despite the obstacles, setbacks, fatigue and feelings of despair, pain and fear produces inner stability and growing confidence in yourself.

Building a career is a creative process: That is, you are creating your life, aren't you? The process of building a career, like any creative development, entails anxiety and uncertainty, and involves fears and self-doubt along with passion and a quest for meaning. The mere knowledge that anxiety and doubt are part of the deal is half a solution. Remember that facing any task under uncertain conditions requires trusting the process. Steve Jobs called it "connecting the dots." This is what he said in his famous Stanford speech:

> *You can't connect the dots looking forward; you can only connect them looking backwards. So you have to trust that the dots will somehow connect in your future. You have to trust in something – your gut, destiny, life, karma, whatever. This approach has never let me down, and it has made all the difference in my life.*

Ask! Do not be afraid to ask. People are afraid to ask because of fear of rejection and refusal, or due to an inner belief that "I don't deserve it." The fact is that if you ask you might get it (or not), but if you do not ask – you won't get it for sure. Right after I left my job as manager of a Pilates studio, they opened a Pilates instructor training program in which I wanted to enroll. I had no means of paying for the course, and I decided to ask whether I could take it for free even though I no longer worked there. I contacted my ex-employer and – much to my surprise – she agreed.

Deal with objections: Anxiety has a powerful way of giving rise to objections. Suddenly there're an awful lot of important things that need taking care of – the house is dirty, there are dishes in the sink, there is that call to make to the plumber. I'm always amazed at how facing unpleasant tasks is a great impetus to get me clean the house. Do you recognize this?

Sometimes our body joins the chorus of objections with pain, fatigue and constipation. These might all be manifestations of resistance. An even more interesting phenomenon is when external reality reflects your anxieties. When I moved into my own apartment for the first time I was very excited but also a little scared. During the first week I had all possible objective reasons why I should not sleep in my new home. One day I had a car accident, and the next my house was flooded by pouring rain. Finally I realized that what was happening around me was an accurate reflection of my resistance and concern.

The way to deal with objections is, first, to identify them as such; second, to reassure yourself that they are only manifestations of your fear of change; and finally, to keep on moving ahead.

Love and forgive yourself if you feel weak and scared. First of all, it's a matter of principle. Weakness or fear do not justify self-hatred. Nothing does. Acceptance of yourself and self-love are conditions for happiness and success in life, and they are, in fact, more important than money, success, and even happiness. We all have a little child inside us who gets excited about some things and is terrified of other things. Adulthood is about respecting, not rejecting, that little child. Simply say to yourself: "I forgive you for being afraid, for being weak. I love you unconditionally."

You might ask yourself: Doesn't accepting something mean settling for less? If I accept an undesirable situation does that mean I give up on changing it? It is always surprising to find out that it is the other way around. **If we accept a situation it becomes easier to change it.**

Forgiving yourself is not manipulation; it is a true act of understanding, acceptance and compassion and ultimately love for yourself. But it certainly can make a real difference.

The Anger Process: This technique was introduced by Dr. John Gray in his book *What You Feel, You Can Heal*, and it's instrumental in harnessing anger's warm energy in favor of positive change. The foundation of anger is positive; under all existing anger lies desire, and beneath desire lies a sense of self-worth and self-love. The Anger Process is a way to come back home to the positive source of anger, in a manner not unlike following a path of bread crumbs in the forest.

The Anger Process includes three steps: the first step is getting angry with yourself. Look in the mirror and tell yourself all the things about yourself that make you disappointed, angry or bitter. You can say things like: "I hate you because you are so scared when …," "I'm disappointed that you're acting like a chicken when …," and so on. Address yourself in the second person ("I'm mad at you") and not the first ("I'm mad at myself"). Use an angry voice. Allow yourself to throw unprocessed charges and blame. After 2-3 minutes move on to the second step.

In the second step become your own motivator. Express your wishes for yourself using the same angry and assertive tone. For example: "I want you to grow up," "I want you to really succeed," "I want you to express yourself," "I want you to calm down" and so forth. This stage also takes about 2-3 minutes.

In the third and final stage be your own cheerleader. Encourage yourself with the same bursting energy and firm voice. Use positive and supportive statements. For example: "You can do it," "You deserve to succeed," "I love your courage and determination," "I love you," "You can do it."

The Anger Process may sound contradictory to forgiveness and self-love, but it is not. In my experience, sometimes the best way to approach difficulty is through softness and compassion, and sometimes it's through a firm and energetic attitude. Choose the most suitable approach for you at the moment.

Treat fear as a friend: Try to treat fear as a signpost that reads: "Caution! Border Crossing Ahead!" Be curious about this border, and make it a regular practice to cross it from time to time.

Love & Freedom

" *"Without work, all life goes rotten,*
but when work is soulless, life stifles and dies" "

(Albert Camus)

Are you really aiming for a career you love?

Let's do some quick math: take an average working week of 40 hours and you get 2010 hours spent working in a year. That's a considerable amount of time by any measure. Many people will put effort into giving careful attention to planning their time on a weekend out-of-town, yet they willingly swallow the idea of long and unsatisfactory working hours (at best) or a deep sense of frustration and bitterness (at worst).

"One cannot combine pleasure with work." "Enjoyment is reserved for leisure and hobbies." "Life is not a picnic." "You cannot make a living from hobbies." "Work as an extension of passion is nice in theory but, in reality, life is hard. One should be realistic." These are just some of the statements I often hear. Many people give up their right to work and earn a living from doing what they love. As I mentioned in the introduction to this book, according to a survey by the company Right Management, only 19% of employees in the United States and Canada say they are satisfied with their jobs.

Do you work doing what you love or have you given up on fulfilling your professional dreams? Do you settle for work being merely a source of income, and relegate your favorite pastimes and hobbies to your leisure time?

Dr. Tal Ben-Shahar writes in his book *Happier* that although career change may seem daunting, it is necessary if our current work provides only for our material needs. Suggesting a mental exercise, he turns the tables and asks: If we found ourselves in a job that didn't provide for our elementary material needs, we would definitely make every effort to solve the problem. So why do we set lower standards when our happiness is at stake?

A good question, isn't it?

Work can be a passionate and pleasurable activity, one that adds a twinkle to your eye, and fills life with meaning and satisfaction. 2010 hours of passion and meaning in a year is worth demanding.

EXERCISE:
Are you on the career path you really like and want?

Do you know what you want to do? The following questions will help you identify hidden dreams:

What would I do if unlimited options were open to me, and there were no economic or social restrictions?

What would I do for the rest of my life, even if I weren't getting paid a

single dollar for it?

If I lived in Sweden/New Zealand/Monaco, what kind of job would I choose? (This question is designed to bypass social constraints, so the idea is to pick a country with a culture unfamiliar to you).

*Some of your answers could or would seem like far-fetched fantasies – for example, being a restaurant critic or writing prose or even being a lion tamer. Right now it does not matter. The goal of your first step is to **identify** your desires, and allow yourself to dream. It could be that you feel you are delusional and are giving yourself false hope. Maybe you are afraid that if you allow yourself to dream, you will wake up one morning and end up living your life in a reality of dangerous and irresponsible adventure. Stand reassured: no one is asking you to change your life. No need to do anything. At this stage we are only exploring. The goal is to get to know yourself better.*

Enjoyment and success

Do you believe that money and pleasure are two separate matters? Despite the common perception that sets pleasure and livelihood apart from each other, various specialists and researchers claim that the facts indicate otherwise. Choosing a profession that you truly love is a reasonable proposition, economically speaking.

Several years ago, when I worked in an administrative position that depressed me, I came across the book *The 80/20 Principle* by Richard Koch. He wrote the following: "Specialize in a field you're interested in and you enjoy. You cannot become leaders and gain recognition without enthusiasm and a strong desire ... enthusiasm motivates personal achievements and is infectious, thus creating a multiplier effect. It is impossible to fake or create enthusiasm." In other words, you can only excel and therefore really succeed in that which you truly enjoy.

Thinking back, I knew that producing spreadsheet reports didn't excite me, but I thought that engaging in writing or starting my own business was too big a risk. Nevertheless, at that stage of my life I knew from experience that I could not persevere with something that bored me. During most of my adult life I had chosen "safe" lines of work which I had not liked, so I quit them sooner or later, and therefore couldn't pave a career path that would substantially advance me . Deep inside I did not really want to excel in those jobs. I was depressed by the idea that I was stuck deep in the mud and was good at it! Koch's words struck a chord with me. I decided to adopt his approach, and looked for ways to engage in what truly uplifted and excited me.

Most employment consultants first examine one's talents and abilities, and then they examine one's heart's desires. But passion and enthusiasm are essential to produce really extraordinary work. Koch argues that most people who climbed to the top in their field were those who were really passionate about their work. Passion is not a feeling that work "is fine," but rather a feeling that your work turns you on, and excites and interests you, and that you are happy to talk about it with anyone who will listen. Nothing really great is achieved without passion, because without it you lack the sufficiently strong motivation to do what it takes to succeed. When you really know what you want to do, when you crave it, there is no limit to your tenacity and determination. Even if you sometimes choose jobs out of consideration for convenience or financial security, your passion will gnaw at you and it won't let you silence it for too long. Passion is your compass, the engine that makes you get up in the morning and continue to insist, to fight for yourself. It is your shield in the face of setbacks, disappointments and crises.

When you genuinely love what you do, then the "work" and "hobbies" dichotomy conjoins. You do what you love, and you love what you do. Rachel, a bakery owner, says: "I get up in the morning and do not feel like I'm going to work. I do what I love and I get paid for it. For me it's a dream come true."

The road to success: pleasure, satisfaction, and talent

A fitting job, says Ben-Shahar, should reflect the following three factors:

1.   Pleasure (passion).
2.   Satisfaction and meaning (giving value).
3.   Capability (talent).

Similarly, researchers Thompson, Emery and Porras claim in their book *Success Built to Last* that success of the most long-lasting and thriving organizations is based on three P's: Passion, Purpose, and Performance. Passion refers to your vision and your right to pursue it. Purpose stands for the value you give to others and identification with a goal bigger than yourself. Performance refers to the practical actions you take to transform your goal into practice.

We have already talked about passion. Let's take a look into the two other factors: giving value and talent.

Giving value; fulfilling your calling

An important factor in finding the right job for you is giving value. That is, giving others something which is deeply meaningful. Touching others in ways that move and satisfy you profoundly. Some people (e.g. comedians, hospital clowns, event producers) experience deep satisfaction from making other people happy. Others (e.g. couples' and family therapists) derive satisfaction from improving people's relationships. There are also some (e.g. engineers, architects) who are inspired and satisfied by planning and constructing facilities that will serve individuals and businesses. Yet others (e.g. doctors, veterinarians, holistic therapists) draw satisfaction from curing diseases and saving lives.

Giving value is where your skills meet meaning. The highest level of satisfaction is achieved when you are exceptionally talented in what you do. You give others the most precious gift you can, the one you were born to give. Giving to others that which results from your extreme talent and what you enjoy doing will enrich your life with satisfaction and meaning. You might feel that this is your calling.

The psychologist Amy Wrzesniewski and her colleagues studied the different ways employees relate to their work. They found that employees who considered their work a calling believed that their undertakings made the world a better place. People who saw their work as a calling spent more time engaging in their vocation, whether they were paid for it or not, and drew more pleasure and satisfaction from it than employees who saw their work only as a source of income or personal advancement. One of the most interesting findings established by Wrzesniewski and her colleagues is that employees who considered their jobs as callings drew more satisfaction from their work than from hobbies and leisure activities. In general, the work of employees with a sense of calling also reflected their passion.

However, your contribution must be significant for you. "The biggest contribution I can give," said a friend "arises from self-love." That is, whatever is satisfying and pleasurable, meaningful and passionate for you. Doing just that thing (or things) that really increases your passion and engages your unique abilities can give you a sense of freedom. Ben-Shahar argues: "We are experiencing a sense of freedom when we **choose** a path which provides us with both meaning and pleasure." [Emphasis in the original.] Our world is full of people whose hearts and talents are inclined in one direction and yet they do something else: poets who work as managers, therapists who work in marketing, fashion designers who teach languages. But there is no substitute for a career that matches your personality and capabilities. The career counselor Barbara Sher claims in her book *I Could Do Anything, If Only I Knew What It Was:*

> *Real meaning, your kind of meaning, is as pure and unique as you were as a child ... When you're doing the right work you will feel connected, both to your soul and to the world outside*

you ... When something really matters to you, you must bring it into your life.

Your will also make back your contribution multiplied many times over. When you make good on your talents, you not only bestow upon others but also evolve and open yourself up to new knowledge. When I write, coach or work with groups I often feel inspired. Various spiritual teachers and creators report that the experience of creating or giving is a tool for achieving inspiration and abundance. Within your act of giving, you are a tool imparting knowledge and wisdom that benefits your clients. The source of that knowledge is muse, inspiration or divine spark, you name it. When you give, you receive. I am painfully aware of my own need to give or create for my own sake; because this is the only way I can continue to grow.

Providing value and financial gain

President John F. Kennedy said: "Ask not what your country can do for you, ask what you can do for your country." Examine your beliefs regarding success: Do you believe that the strongest will always win? That chasing dollars will make you richer? Or, rather, that giving to others can increase your revenue? One of the paradoxes of success is: **giving value generates money**. Define your service in terms of the value you offer and not in terms of how much money you will gain. If you give tremendous value, the money will follow.

Rami Levy, one of Israel's most accomplished businessmen, advised business owners at a conference in April 2013: "Any enterprise that runs for long distances should reflect on a daily basis about how it benefits the consumer it is serving. This way it will always be on the path to success." The logic behind this notion is solid and down-to-earth: the way to build a thriving business is to make sure you have clients who are avid fans. The best way to guarantee yourself avid fans is to give them abundant value. In their groundbreaking book *Built to Last*, which reveals the common denominators of 18 truly exceptional and long-lasting organizations, Jim Collins and Jerry Porras refute the most common and conventional perceptions in business management. For example, **they found that visionary companies are not interested primarily in money,** and that companies with vision never change their core values. Business coaches Eran Stern and Alon Ulman call this the Law of Compensation, stating that your economic worth is directly proportional to the value you give. As you give more value to more people your income level will rise. Thus the best way to increase your income is to ask yourself: "How can I give much more value to many more people today?" The definition of value is simple: you provide value when you leave a person in a better place than when you first met them.

You need to recognize and define your value, your unique contribution – and live your life confirming this. I find that this challenge – "How can I provide more value to people today?" – helps me do my best and pilots me to strive for precision in my work.

EXERCISE:
What value do you give?

Ask yourself regarding your career: How does my target benefit others? Your target might be to improve quality of life, or to heal, or inspire, or help others reach their potential, and so forth.
To what extent do you personally identify with this goal? Does it excite you? What is your bonus added value in your field? Formulate it clearly, accurately and concisely.

Fear of desire:
My dream is stupid, harmful or dangerous

Does your work fill you with joy, passion, satisfaction and meaning? Do you feel that your work is a manifestation of your unique talents? If so, you are definitely on the right path. Many people settle for jobs that are just "OK" for them. Sometimes they do not even know what they want to do – or else they do know but prematurely dismiss the chance to realize their dream.

Naomi, a woman in her 30s, joined a career-change workshop after a difficult and painful divorce following years in a miserable marriage. "What's your dream?" I asked her. "What burns inside you?" "Nothing," she replied. "I do not want anything. I learned to put my dreams on hold. I have no more strength for disappointments." Naomi is an example of a person who chooses to bury her desires. Many people, like Naomi, do not even know what they want to do. They learned that dreaming is dangerous, that love hurts and that attempts at self-expression lead to rejection and failure. Other people know what they want but are afraid to realize their dreams. To the onlooker, it seems that they fill their time with many activities, while neglecting to advance themselves and their aspirations.

Why does this happen?

Fear of hurting your loved ones

Some people do not dare connect to their desires or fulfill their own wishes because one of their parents (or both) is frustrated and professionally unfulfilled. They are concerned (albeit unconsciously) that success or professional development would be a painful reminder of the parent's having missed out. These people choose to identify with the parent's failure in order to protect the mother or father from renewed pain. They find it difficult to accept compliments and feel guilty about accomplishments because they have learned that they come at the expense of others.

One such case is Becky, who came from a family "heritage" of women who had all worked in simple, production-line jobs, and, once they married, stopped working altogether. Becky lived with her infirm mother and was afraid that if she realized her capabilities, or even left home, that it would be at the expense of her dependent parent. Consequently, she had no professional aspirations. Her personal desires were completely shoved aside by the strong sense of commitment she harbored towards her mother.

Examine your close environment. Are any of the people who are closest and most important to you either frustrated, discouraged or unfulfilled professionally? If this is indeed the case, you may have relinquished your right to succeed. Relationships based on frustration and mutual sacrifice foster unhealthy dependency, anger and resentment. It's very difficult to grow within such a relationship. Your frustration is not beneficial to those close to you, and it is very harmful to you.

Despair: "I lose everything anyway"

Some people live with a feeling that dreaming, wanting and loving are dangerous and painful. People who have experienced traumatic or multiple separations, deaths and changes of residence may develop a sense that nothing of value lasts for long. They may lose their will to invest effort and time in meaningful and sustainable productivity. Intense unprocessed pain over past losses casts a heavy shadow on the present.

Naomi's case, which I mentioned earlier in this chapter, is one such illustration. Naomi's father abandoned her when she was a child, and her longing for the absent father had a profound impact on her life. In adulthood, she married an abusive man who humiliated and beat her. Since she had experienced love as something that elicits pain and heartbreak, she was afraid to rededicate herself. She learned to expect little from life, and was afraid to dream about a fulfilling profession and of feeling real passion. Fear that her dream would be shattered and that her heart would break again paralyzed her ability to dream.

Wanting is prohibited or dangerous

Maybe you received the message in your early years that having desires is selfish and inconsiderate. You learned to be a "good kid," to please others and take care of them. You learned that good children better do what they are asked to do, answer when they are asked and fulfill all their duties. You may have suffered angry, critical and even ridiculing reactions when you tried to express yourself, your wishes and your talents. If your desires were perceived as rebellion, caprice or just plain silly ideas, you might have learned to suppress your desires and give up the right to dream. Children's need to receive approval and love from their environment is so existential and essential to their survival that it surmounts the need for self-expression. Today, you do not know what you want; or you do know, but suffer from low self-esteem, don't believe in your abilities, are scared to express yourself, and fear that you will "catch hell" if you attempt to emerge from your quiet corner.

People who put off their desires and aspirations often excel at taking care of others, but they do a poor job taking care of themselves. They may be hardworking, loyal and dedicated family members and employees, but they find it difficult to leverage themselves and promote their own needs and wishes. A particular example is Ethan, a cinematography teacher. One of Ethan's friends is a well-known screenwriter and film director who has received many international accolades. "He was always talented," Ethan testified, "even twenty-some years ago when we studied cinema together. Like him, I was among the most creative and promising students," he added wistfully. "Now I've got some great scripts in my drawer, but I am constantly busy promoting other people's projects instead of my own."

EXERCISE:
The price of dreams – what scares me?
And, letting go of past baggage

If you find it difficult to identify what you want, or you know what you want but cannot seem to realize it, then you'd probably be better off looking into the fears and other emotions that underlie your being stuck. You can do this by honestly answering the price-tag question:
"What would happen if I pursue something I love? What am I afraid will happen if I succeed? What price would I pay if I fulfill my desires?"

You might answer these questions through free writing in your emotions journal or talking to a friend/family member/professional, but the most important thing is to listen to the most accurate and emotionally authentic answer.

For example, "If I succeed I'm afraid that will hurt so-and-so ..." This is a typical answer for those whose parents were frustrated professionally, and they fear arousing envy or pain if they were to succeed where their parents had failed. Another possible answer could reflect fear of loneliness: "In order to fulfill my desires I would need to give up my relationship with so-and-so ..." This statement is typical for people who grew up in families that required obedience and dependence that frustrated the child's efforts to express his/ her independent personality. The child learned that independence equals emotional abandonment. Alternatively, this statement can surface in a couple's relationship in which one's being stuck serves the needs of the other partner.

Identification of the fear is the first step towards resolution.

Another process that will help you identify and release redundant family baggage or relationship dynamics is to imagine the following situation: Your mother, father, siblings and other significant family figures gather together and say the following words to you:

> *"We accept you just as you are. We understand that our expectations and attitudes have limited you in various ways, and today we want to let you go free. Whatever you decide to do, we will stand behind you. We will love you and support any professional or personal choice you make."*

Now, after you imagine yourself being released from superfluous family baggage, what do you choose to do? What new horizons open up to you?

Limiting beliefs regarding career

People whose "forward gear" has been blocked or hindered sometimes do know what they want to do and are passionate about, but they are afraid to realize it. They think "It's stupid," "There is no money in it," and "It's unfeasible." Reuben, for instance, was an unemployed computer engineer who couldn't find a job. It seemed he had no motivation to return to work as a computer engineer. "Don't get me wrong. I enjoy my profession, but it's not as exciting or thrilling to me as it used to be. I know I have to go back to work but I cannot find the drive to open up the classified ads and send out CVs." A little more in-depth investigation revealed that Reuben had always wanted to study science, and his dream was to become a physicist. When he talked about studying physics, his otherwise tired, listless eyes sparkled. "But ..." and his shoulders sagged, "there's no use talking about it. The studies are demanding and take several years. I would barely be able to work and support my family. It's clearly unrealistic."

Similarly to Reuben, one of my best friends (say her name is Iris) works as a sales manager in a big fashion company, but her dream is to be a farmer. "But it is not profitable," she says, "and I have other priorities in life right now. I'm not ready to give up my standard of living to grow tomatoes."
Iris could be right that her dream is really not worthwhile from a monetary perspective. But, the thing is that Iris and Reuben, like many people, suffer from the **Or Syndrome**. It's a concept that you have either money and prosperity, or you have satisfaction and meaning. The two aspects cannot go hand in hand.

I guess you know the Or Syndrome from either your own life or someone else's. I'm sure you know people who believe that there really is no way to have your cake and eat it too; we either work very hard, make money and live financially comfortable lives, or we quit the rat race and choose relaxed and modest yet financially insecure lives. The Or Syndrome might characterize your way of thinking; you feel you have to choose between your current life (even if you are not that passionate about what you do) and leaving everything behind and chasing your dream.

Collins and Porras discuss this very concept in their book *Built to Last;* people's belief that things can be either A or B but not both. They call it the Tyranny of the OR. They argue that what characterizes successful companies is liberation from the Tyranny of the OR; these find a way to achieve A **and** B at the same time and all the time. For example, if a decision has to be made in favor of low cost or high quality, these companies find a way to reduce costs and maintain high quality. That is, they do the impossible (as it seems to our preconceived OR perception). They manage to have their cake and eat it too.

It is awfully hard to achieve goals we don't believe we really can achieve. If you think there's no chance you'll find a job that you love and also make a living from it, the chance that you will are slim. That is the reason it's important to pinpoint the limiting notions you have about work, love and money, so that you know what limits you and so you can open your mind to new directions in thinking. When you release limiting concepts and believe there is a way to both enjoy what you do and make money, you could find your way there.

EXERCISE:
Changing beliefs and perceptions regarding work

Part A:

Write down the following sentence:
I love my job, and I make my living from it easily and abundantly.

Now write quickly and associatively all objections to this statement that pop up in your mind. For example: "Nonsense, it cannot be," or "I'll never have a job I love."

This exercise will help you uncover the limiting beliefs that block you from finding your ideal life's work.

Part B:

Write down the following headlines:
Career. Money. Career and relationships. Career and leisure. Career and love. *(You are welcome to add any other title that you feel may evoke a reaction from you.)*

Underneath each headline freely write down all the negative beliefs you have about it.

You might feel that some of your statements are not limiting beliefs, but facts. All I ask is that you keep an open and curious mind about those statements, and ask yourself: Really? Does it have to be that way?

In most cases, for each sentence you write there is someone out there who lives in exactly the opposite way. This is a fact.

Why shouldn't it work for you as well?

Part C:

Invert each sentence from negative to positive. For example, if you wrote: "I can never make money from what I love to do," turn it into: "I make an abundant living from what I love to do." If you wrote: "Career women neglect their children," flip in into: "Career women devote more time to their children."

Write the positive statements together on one page and read them every day when you wake up and when you go to bed. Ponder them during the day for at least three weeks.

Give your brain fresh ways of looking at reality.

Values:
Does your work match your personality?

Often the first and foremost step in identifying your career path is to identify what you do not want to do. If you don't know or aren't sure which job suits you, you can begin by defining what is not right for you. Defining the "No" might unlock the door to discovering the "Yes."

A few years ago a woman named Esther came to one of my workshops. She held a position as an administrative director in a government organization and enjoyed earning a nice salary. But Esther felt stifled and unsatisfied. She knew she wanted to leave her current job, but was locked into a rigid two-year contract. If she left, she would have to pay a hefty fine of several thousand dollars.

During the workshop there were some exercises to identify the participants' most significant values. Esther discovered hers to be helping others, creativity and empathy. These values also manifested themselves during the workshop; Esther stood out with the good advice she gave to the other participants along with her high empathetic skills. However, those values were rarely put into practice in her job as an administrative director; her role was more executive than creative, and she managed tasks more than she managed people. Esther looked with frustration at her list of values, and she was visibly shaken. She suddenly realized how far her life had veered away from how she would like it to be. She recognized vividly how her current job inhibited her and made it difficult for her to be the person she wanted to be.

When talking about dissatisfaction at work, we usually mean that your job does not require you to manifest your talents, that the work you produce does not reflect your skill. But the deepest frustration doesn't stem from the fact that you want to paint and instead find yourself fixing refrigerators, but rather from something much deeper – a conflict between your work and your set of values. **Values refer to your state of being – from which your occupation should be derived** – and living according to values means being the person you want to be. When work contradicts who we want to be, we inevitably harbor an inner conflict and suffer from what we do.

Esther's case is a typical example of a career that does not suit one's set of values. She easily recognized that her most important values were creativity, helping others and empathy, but these did not come to fruition in her working life, and she was frustrated. Another example, examined in the wonderful book *Career Your Passion* by the occupational psychologist Dr. Orenia Yaffe-Yanai, is the story of David, a shell-shocked veteran, who had been unable to rebuild his professional life in the twenty years following his duty in the 1973 Yom-Kippur War. During the war David suffered from a series of traumas in which he repeatedly witnessed his friends being killed before his eyes, while he was the only one who survived. David now worked nights in a poultry slaughterhouse in a job he hated and considered pointless, and which was far beneath his abilities. David's dream before the war had been to become a doctor and improve people's health, but instead he found himself working in a field that embodied the very opposite of everything he had aspired to; rather than therapy, he chose to engage with death.

As David progressed in his psychological treatment, his first tangible step towards creating meaningful productivity was opening a petting zoo for children in the yard of his home. This was the same David who once, as a hurt and shell-shocked adult, chose to send animals to slaughter, and was now reconnecting to the child who loved animals and wanted to take care of them.

David's story is a chilling and heart-wrenching example of the potentially enormous gap between one's professional choice and one's values. The bigger a contradiction between values and actions, the deeper the suffering. Conversely, the more consistent one's professional choice is with one's values, the better one's work fills life with substance. **Choosing to lead a life congruent with your set of values is choosing a life of growth and self-realization, and being the person you wish to be.**

If you have chosen an occupation that is inconsistent with your world of values, that choice is not accidental. In David's case it turned out that his feelings of anger, fear and guilt hurt his natural desire to engage in meaningful activity and impaired his emotional ability to realize his original aspiration to heal people. People like David who harbor pent-up anger, fear and guilt often "go on strike" or declare "open rebellion" against life; they hurt themselves and act out their anger on others (and themselves) by avoiding significant productivity.

In the chapters on anger, guilt, loss and fear, I discussed some examples of cases in which a career decision (or indecision) is a manifestation of anger, guilt and fears that need to be addressed. However, in my experience, the very awareness of an inner conflict between work and one's values-world can motivate change. In the case of Esther, for example, when she realized how big the gap was between her professional life and the person she wanted to be, she felt obliged to make a change. At the end of the workshop she hired a good lawyer who helped her leave her job in the government organization. About a year later she opened a photography studio, and later on she also became a therapist, a choice that undoubtedly realized Esther's values.

I would like to add another point: **Values are not just a lighthouse that helps navigate to safe shore, but also the source of our strength.** Consider Simon, who came to counseling in order to sort out his professional life and find more peace. We discovered not only that peacefulness was one of his principal values, but also that when Simon was peaceful he was able to advance important goals; during periods when he was meditating regularly he said, "Miracles happen to me."

Living according to your set of values is a life of inner freedom. You feel you are doing the right thing and following a direction you really enjoy and that truly matches your personality.

FIVE INCARNATIONS EXERCISE:
Identify your set of values

When I say "values" I'm referring to the unique set of qualities that are most significant to you. You might ask: "But some values, say, peace, love and courage are surely important to anyone?" And you are right. However, when people define their 5 to 10 most important values, each person chooses an individual set of values, almost like a personal signature, a digest that expresses their unique personality. For example, one person's most significant set of values might be: creativity, interpersonal relationships, influence, emotional expression and peacefulness. The elected set of values for another person could be: leadership, pleasure, simplicity, intuition and courage.

Write down the following question:
If I could choose five alternative lives – what would I choose to be?

You may pick different occupations (e.g., cowboy, dancer, fortune-teller, monk, scuba diver, policeman, writer, actor, painter, teacher, scientist, UN worker, lion tamer, fisherman, priest, prime minister, car mechanic, housewife, beach lifeguard) or alternative or imaginary life forms (e.g., a mouse, an ant, a man, a woman, a flower, an alien, an invisible observer).

Be specific and elaborate why you chose each of the five incarnations. For example, suppose you choose to be a political journalist with an international online column as one of your incarnations. You have selected this life because exposing the truth is important to you, you value courage and integrity, and you want to have an impact on society. In this case, the values that emerge from this selection are: truth, courage, integrity and leadership.

Extract all the values that emerge from your five selected incarnations. Pick your 5 to 10 most significant values.

Ask yourself how much your real life in general, and in particular, your career life is congruent with your identified values: Assign each value a ranking between 1 and 10. (1 = I don't manifest this value at all in real life. 10 = I fully realize this value in my life.)

Now, ask yourself how your life would look if each value in your list was ranked at 8.

Finally, ask yourself what you can do to increase each value by 20%. Assess this based on supporting factors in your physical environment (place of residence, nutrition, and home arrangement), your lifestyle and your relationships.

*Values can also be derived from your professional vision (read more details on building a career vision in the chapter on happiness). The reason I include the five incarnations exercise here is because it functions like a laser beam pointing precisely to the values that are **currently** most significant to you. If you do this exercise again two years from now, it is most likely you will choose other occupations or life forms that indicate a slightly different set of values. In other words, this exercise helps identify what's missing in your life right now.*

Follow the trail of your passion

Perhaps some of the occupations you listed in the exercise above reflect your fantasies. For instance, living as a monk in an Indian ashram, being an international star singer, or residing on a remote farm and growing tomatoes. Desirable and sometimes impossible fantasies are mirror images of our present life. The more the current life is narrow and pressing, the more dangerous, wild and far-reaching the dream will be. One example is Nathaniel, who worked as production manager in a high-tech company. When I asked him what he would do in another lifetime, he said he would like to be a world-famous DJ. I recommended to Nathaniel, and also recommend to you, to beware of hasty steps such as "leaving everything behind and chasing my dream." When rekindling your passion, it is important to feel in control, to create clear boundaries, and carefully build tools to contain it.

Instead of taking drastic measures with far-reaching implications in your personal and professional life, I suggest that you start to follow the trail of your passion, materializing your passions in tiny steps. **Reignite the fire in your life by dedicating time and resources to what you love to do within your day-to-day living.**

The ability to enjoy is like a muscle that needs nutrition and exercise. If you don't allow yourself to enjoy today, it will be very difficult for you to encourage yourself to find an enjoyable job tomorrow. A while ago I met a young woman who hated her job and did not know what she wanted to do otherwise. She emphasized that it was important for her to enjoy her vocational choice. I asked her to what extent, on a scale of 1 (lowest) to 10 (highest), she was a person who allowed herself to enjoy. "Five," she replied. I explained to her that in order to find a job she enjoys she must learn to be able to enjoy today! You can start with hobbies, conversations with friends, drawing, nature trips, reading books. I also highly recommend finding ways to enjoy more things in your present job. Whether by diversifying your job responsibilities, branching out at your current place of work, or even by making small changes in your work environment (like hanging family pictures and listening to music).

There is a Buddhist saying: "If you want to keep a drop from drying up – throw it into the sea." Similarly, if you want desire to motivate you, you must ignite it on a regular basis. Passion is an attitude towards life.

One of the best ways to follow your dreams, even if you do not fully know what you want to do, is to follow the trail of your passion. Each small step of doing what you love will bring you closer to the next significant action. Like in the story of Hansel and Gretel, your "passion path" is a trail of pebbles that will take you home.

In one part of *The Neverending Story* by Michael Ende, the protagonist, Bastian, has a serious talk about the meaning of the words "Do what you wish" with the lion Grograman (also known as the Many Colored Death). Grograman explains the meaning and importance of following one's heart:

> *Bastian had shown the lion the inscription on the reverse side*
> *of the Gem. "What do you suppose it means?" he asked. " 'DO*

WHAT YOU WISH.' That must mean I can do anything I feel like. Don't you think so?"

All at once Grograman's face looked alarmingly grave, and his eyes glowed.

"No," he said in his deep, rumbling voice. "It means that you must do what you really and truly want. And nothing is more difficult."

"What I really and truly want? What do you mean by that?"

"It's your own deepest secret and you yourself don't know it."

"How can I find out?"

"By going the way of your wishes, from one to another, from first to last. It will take you to what you really and truly want."

"That doesn't sound so hard," said Bastian.

"It is the most dangerous of all journeys."

"Why?" Bastian asked. "I'm not afraid."

"That isn't it," Grograman rumbled. "It requires the greatest honesty and vigilance, because there's no other journey on which it's so easy to lose yourself forever ..."

In the days that followed Bastian thought a good deal about what the Many Colored Death had said. There are some things, however, that we cannot fathom by thinking about them, but only by experience. So it was not until much later, after all manner of adventures, that he thought back on Grograman's words and began to understand them.

Follow the cobblestone path of your passion: Enroll in a graphic design course, get up two hours earlier in the morning and write, start a cooking blog, volunteer at an animal shelter, take a course at the Open University. This new hobby or activity might help you fine-tune your professional choice. For example, in her book *A Person Bursts into Flight* Rona Raanan-Shafrir tells the story of a client named Siegel who came for counseling when her career was about to take off. She had completed her Ph.D. and worked her way into the academic world, yet she felt devoid of energy, "like a bag with a hole in it, letting the air out slowly." Siegel felt she had been "living from her waist up all her life," while the lower part of her body – symbolizing sexuality and creativity – was paralyzed. During the counseling process Siegel recalled how much she loved animals, and she adopted two puppies. In addition, she began to walk on a daily basis. Siegel did not leave her academic job, but did renew her contact with other elements within her and the world that related to touch, emotion and body. Later she found a way to combine the worlds of intellect and emotion through a research project on the relationship between dogs and people with perception problems.

In any case, whether or not your hobby will turn into a profession, doing what you love is the first step to plunging into deeper layers of your passion. Listening to the heart is a skill that requires practice. If you follow the trail of your passion, if you take the emotional risk of committing to do what you love, you will finally find your deepest passion and the way to materialize it. The poet Rumi said: "Let yourself be silently drawn by the stronger pull of what you really love. It will not lead you astray." The search itself might fulfill your life passion, love, meaning and bliss.

The power of love

When I was young I believed that in order to be successful people need to be aggressive and fight their way in the world using elbows. Being the third generation in a family of Holocaust survivors (almost all the relatives of my grandparents on both sides were murdered during World War II), I was raised in a "survivors" environment. I grew up believing that only the strong survive, that emotions are expression of weakness, and that aggressive confrontation is often the best way to achieve goals.

One of the life events that made me reconsider this premise was an encounter with … a cat. Several years ago an abandoned cat turned up at my door. I lived in an area where there were many tough and semi-wild street cats. They burrowed through trash, hunted small animals, and led independent lives without human contact. Back then I did not like cats, I regarded them as selfish and unreliable animals, and did not pay them any special attention. In the first few days after she appeared, I considered the new cat a nuisance. I waited for her to leave or start fending for herself, but she obviously did not manage. She was different. She was not as tough as the other cats, but actually sought contact, touch and warmth. Whenever the door was open she tried to come inside the house and snuggle up against me. She didn't go away on hunting trips, but instead waited consistently at the door, meowing from hunger or thirst. As the days passed she got quieter, and I found myself beginning to care for her. I bought her food, brought her water, and began to spend time playing with her and petting her. Eventually I found a caring home for her, and gave her away, not without sorrow.

That this anonymous cat made my heart open up to her got me pondering. I compared her to the other cats; they were tougher and knew their way around. But does that mean they were stronger? Their toughness was also a source of vulnerability. Because they were afraid of people and were aggressive towards humans, they didn't find loving homes, and as a result were more susceptible to street fights, survival battles and premature death. However, that abandoned and vulnerable cat that sought contact and help managed to touch me and create a protected and better life for herself.

That got me thinking about myself. With what language do I speak to the world? Is my toughness a strength or a weakness? Aren't trust, sensitivity and vulnerability even more powerful? I began to believe more in love – in communicating with the world through the language of the heart.

If you listen to your own heart you may find weakness, pain and injuries, but you will also discover that the world reacts to you. If you act out of love, others will be touched and moved as well. Your heart will resonate with other hearts and will get you to places where aggression, survival battles or fear can never take you. A career motivated by self-love and love for others is a terrific way to live in greater harmony with the world.

Realizing your dreams – taking an emotional risk

Passionate life is also life that carries a risk. Loving and realizing your love involves taking an emotional risk because pursuing your passions touches on intense emotions, pain and vulnerability. When you dare to realize a dream you might also feel pain or get hurt and disappointed. There is something safe about dreaming big, about the distant fantasy: "When I retire I will finally ..." "When my children grow up I will have time to pursue my dreams ..." The everyday routine remains mundane and gray, and you can continue to dream that one day your life will take a turn. There's no risk to it. You do not put your dream to the test, do not express your special talents, do not run the risk of rejection, do not risk disappointment, and do not need to think about possible criticism.

The greatest risk in pursuing dreams is not the financial one. There is hardly a dream that can't be realized in everyday life. For example, Franz Kafka, one of the most influential authors of the 20th century, was an insurance employee most of his life. Martin Aylward, an international Buddhist meditation teacher, got married and had children at a young age, so he never retreated as a monk for long periods as do most teachers. Allon Kira, one of Israel's leading macro photographers, developed his career and opened a photography school while continuing to hold his day job as an accountant.

The greatest risk is really the emotional one. When I decided to pursue my artistic dream I enrolled in an evening music school. I remember stepping out of the fantasy of a singing career into a routine of breathing exercises, diction lessons and singing in a choir. I no longer sang only in the shower. I experienced the tremors and stomach palpitations. I began to compare myself to other singers and appraise whether I was good and to what extent. In other words, I put my dream to a test. The most precious thing I could give to others – my heart, soul and passion – was no longer a private dream, but out on stage and in the public eye. I was subjected to self-criticism and received feedback from others, and eventually found I was only a mediocre vocalist. At first, when my dream shattered in the face of reality, I did experience a crisis, but putting my dream to a test had made me dive in to look deeper into my dreams. I discovered my passion for singing was not really that strong, but was rather a screen on my will to express myself, move and touch others. I realized I wanted to work with people in development and empowerment processes.

So whether you find that your dream fills you with passion and you are determined to achieve it, or whether you discover that it is not for you, you win in any case. You make another major step towards self-realization.

Freedom of choice:
Getting pleasure from the profession you love

Sylvie chose a profession she loved – being a life coach. The coaching profession embodied her desire to help others with her creativity and her need for independence. Sylvie became a coach after ten years of working as a schoolteacher:

> *I chose to be a teacher because everyone said it was a good profession for women. I never gave it much thought. My mom is a schoolteacher too, so ... But I realized pretty quickly that it was not for me. Discipline issues never really appealed to me. And teaching a class of thirty five children is not exactly the pinnacle of education in my opinion. I also hated the fact that I had to teach a fixed syllabus which occasionally bored not only me but the children as well. Besides, I always knew I preferred working with adults. After ten years of teaching, when I saw that I was angry and resentful and I realized that the children had gotten on my nerves, I finally resolved to make a change. I decided to become a life coach because I knew that I had a lot to give, and I'm not subject to this or that agenda. I am creative and*

focused and enjoy working with grownups who are committed to themselves.

Sylvie's career choice to become a life coach stemmed from maturity and sorting out her needs and desires. However, something still did not work. Although she loved her profession, she could not enjoy her daily work routine. She mainly had difficulty managing her time effectively, and balancing work and family. She worked over ten hours a day, and found it hard to break away from the phone and emails even when sitting at a family meal. She felt the business was "taking over my life." Sylvie was exhausted and full of guilt towards her husband and children. She felt she didn't enjoy her job, even though she knew she had wisely chosen a profession that she truly loved and which fulfilled her skill set.

Like Sylvie, you may have chosen your dream profession but everyday life is not a field of dreams. You are encumbered by multitasking, you feel tense and overloaded, and you do not feel the sense of freedom you expected to be inherent in a realization of your vision. Maybe you feel like the psychiatrist and writer Irvin Yalom depicts in one of his books, that sometimes he feels as if he's being chased with a gun to perform his job. Difficulty in enjoying your chosen productivity, feelings of stress, fear of failure, ineffective time management and the need to please others are common to many people. You are indeed lucky because you know what you want to do, and have found your calling, but you cannot enjoy the fruits of your labor. Instead of feeling that you control your life, you feel that you are chasing your own tail. You feel enslaved to work. Sylvie's way to describe this situation was: "I feel like I've reached a well, but I cannot drink from it."

The question is how to add the quality of freedom into work? How to work without feeling suffocated? How to find a way to enjoy self-fulfillment?

The answer lies in a deeper understanding of the concept of "freedom of choice" which I think is one of the important features of self-love. Freedom of choice is the ability to determine your goals, choose how to manage your time, and be the "boss" of your own life. The groundbreaking psychologist Donald

Winnicott called freedom of choice "a creative approach" and saw it as an indicator of good mental health. According to Winnicott, a creative approach is an expression of internal freedom, a sense of control, free choice and finding meaning in life; a feeling that life is worth living. According to his perception, the opposite of the creative experience is submission to the outside world, a feeling that external reality is something that one should adapt to, and a sense of futility and doubt about the value of life. Winnicott, many of whose writings deal with creativity and its importance in individuals' lives from infancy to adulthood, said:

> *I am hoping that the reader will accept a general reference to creativity, not letting the word get lost in the successful or acclaimed creation, but keeping it to the meaning that refers to a coloring of the whole attitude to external reality.*

You could say that Winnicott regarded life as a big lump of clay, and the creative approach is the freedom to play with this clay, act upon it and shape it according to one's own world. Therefore, he argues that "it is only in being creative that the individual discovers the self."

Sylvie, whose story was presented earlier in this chapter, realized that her difficulty in enjoying her work was that she was not really emotionally free or creative enough in managing her schedule. As a schoolteacher she had to accept the dictates of the system and syllabus. She was subject to the guidelines and instructions of the school management and the Ministry of Education. As a teacher she was part of a system with very specific laws under which she had to operate. When Sylvie opened her own business, she had indeed enjoyed great autonomy in terms of hours, choice of clients, professional approach and so on, but she acted as if she was still subject to external dictates:

> *It's as if I had internalized the education system into my life. While it was I who set my daily schedule, I did it in a rigid style and without much consideration for my own needs. My days were overbooked with meetings. I hardly gave myself time to rest. I was afraid to say 'No' to clients if I was unavailable or*

not interested in working with them. I mean, I had freedom
of choice, but I used it to create a life for myself with a lot of
responsibilities, a little free time, and very little freedom.

Sylvie, who for most of her life was used to abiding by system demands, continued to behave as if there were an external system forcing her to act in a certain way. She wasn't attentive enough to her needs, which included time for reflection, developing her creativity, and time for rest and family.

Self-respect;
taking up the reins of your own life

Freedom of choice or creative approach are largely related to self-respect. I do not mean ego or need for recognition, but a deep respect for yourself, your feelings, your needs and your world view. The National Geographic channel shows a TV program I really like called *Dog Whisperer.* The program features the dog trainer Cesar Millan's work of rehabilitating dogs by reestablishing their relationships with their owners. Millan's basic rule in his work with dog owners is to teach them to act in an assertive but calm, authoritative yet patient manner. Millan explains and consistently demonstrates that a good relationship between people and their dogs results when the owners are the leaders and the dogs follow their authority. The owners must respect themselves for the dogs to consequently respect them. Therefore, a lack of authority on the owner's part adversely affects the behavior of the dog. Only calm and self-confident (vs. aggressive) energy radiated by the owner will impart a sense of security to the dog, teach it to be disciplined, and give it room to be a happy dog and a loyal friend.

Personally, I believe that developing an ability to be authoritative, peaceful and harmonious with a creature with such a proximity to its primal feelings and wild nature (like a dog) helps develop the right attitude towards life. But dogs aside ... this series helped me understand how to "tame" my life. The "right" approach is to take up the reins of my life, assume control, put myself at the center, and establish an authoritative attitude. When I'm attentive to my needs, my environment responds positively to me. When I am reactive, appeasing and restless, my professional and interpersonal environment becomes chaotic.

Only when I am calm and balanced can I really help others. You could say that people are like musical instruments that produce sounds. Only if we take proper care of the tool (i.e., ourselves) will we be able to produce magical sounds. It's a basic rule of life. We do not serve anyone when we give up on our own needs. The Buddhist teacher Ajahn Chah said: "There is only one seat in my mind and I'm sitting on it." To me, this sentence embodies the meaning of self-respect.

One of the most determined, accomplished and yet self-attentive people I know is Dr. Riky Shai, founder and director of an empowerment center for women. Shai grew up in an immigrant family of limited means, and got married and had two daughters at an early age. Concurrently, she did not give up on her dream to learn and develop. In the early years of her marriage she worked several jobs to finance her tuition and provide for the growing family. During the day she worked at various odd jobs, including cleaning, and at night she wrote academic paper assignments for university. "All this time," she says, "I knew with all my heart that this dark period would pass and the sun would rise and shine on us." Shai completed her teaching certificate and worked as a schoolteacher, gave birth to two more children, completed her Ph.D., established a women's empowerment center, and then went into politics.

Dr. Shai's determination, activism and high energy are amongst her prominent features, but she has two more characteristics that need to be mentioned: her attentiveness to her own needs and her joie de vivre. Every morning Shai opens her day with a trip to the beach with her dog. She works till noontime, then takes a few hours' break. Every day, from 2:00 to 5:00 p.m., she stays home and is unavailable for meetings or phone calls. This is her time for resting and family. After 5 p.m. she continues to work until nighttime. When Shai ran for the office of mayor, one of her deputy-to-be candidates told her: "When I'm your number two you can forget about your afternoon rest." And she replied:

"You can forget about being my number two." She knew that her own way to manage her busy lifestyle, whilst balancing home and work duties – and maintaining physical and mental health – was keeping her afternoon break, and no one could take it away from her. She was the master of her life; she set her own goals, assumed control over her schedule, and was not afraid to say "No."

In the Self-Esteem chapter I talked about the concept of "attachment." In short, attachment is being enslaved to one's urges and desires, crossing the fine line between passion and obsession. Activity born of passion invigorates and fills life with vivacity and joy. However, when acting upon attachments we become troubled, anxious, fearful of the prospect that we will not achieve our goal, and tired from the excess effort. Passion liberated of attachments always involves qualities of peace and confidence, whether it's confidence in achieving the goal or a general trust in life; that everything is alright. **Passion, by definition, involves recognizing your desires and strengths, whereas peace is actually related to recognizing your limitations,** recognizing the border of what you can or want to do. This combination – recognition of strengths and limitations – creates desire without attachment and allows freedom of choice, pleasure and joy.

Ask yourself: Do your goals energize you or put you down? Are your goals mostly stressful or are they making you happier and fuller with a sense of meaning?

Being assertive and calm in your work – suggestions and tips

Be proactive: Proactivity is the first habit in Stephen Covey's book *The 7 Habits of Highly Effective People*. Being proactive means creating opportunities in life, initiating and bringing about changes. Reactive behavior is to wait for things to happen and then responding to them.

Prioritize: Being proactive is also about focus. Define to yourself the most important goals in your life and focus on them first. Look at the following story as an illustration:

> *One day, an old professor lectured to a group of high-powered managers about efficient time management. 'OK,' he slowly met the eyes of his avid listeners, 'we are going to conduct an experiment.' Then he pulled out a big wide-mouthed glass jar and set it on the table in front of him. Next, he produced a bag of tennis ball-sized stones and carefully placed them, one by one, in the jar.*
>
> *He did this until the jar was filled to the top and no more stones would fit in. 'Is this jar full?' He asked, and the managers replied, 'Yes.' 'Really?' he questioned, and then reached under the table and pulled out a bag of pebbles. The professor poured some pebbles into the jar and carefully shook it, causing the pebbles to slip down through the spaces between the bigger stones.*
>
> *Once again, he smiled and asked the group 'Is the jar full?' By this time the managers began to understand his intentions. 'Probably not,' one of them replied. 'Good!' called the old professor, and pulled out a bag of sand from under the table. Then he poured the sand into the jar, and it filled up all the spaces left between the stones and the pebbles. Yet again, he asked the group: 'Is this jar full?' 'No!' all the managers cried out together. 'Correct!' he replied, and reached for a water-pitcher that was on the table. He poured water into the jar until it was filled to the brim.*
>
> *The old professor now looked up at his audience and asked: 'What is the point of this experiment?'*
>
> *One manager ventured: 'The point is, no matter how full your schedule may appear, you can always squeeze tasks into it, if you only try harder!'*

'No,' replied *the old professor, 'that's not the point. This experiment teaches us something different: If you don't put the larger stones in the jar first, you'll never be able to get all of them in later.'*

Ask yourself: What are the large stones in your life? Are they your relationships? Your career? Your health? If you are reading this book I guess your career is one of those large stones. If so, define the big stones within your career. Which are your favorite clients? Focus on them. What is your added value? Strengthen it. What are your most profitable projects? Invest in them. What steps can you take to propel your career forward? Undertake them.

Nurture peace and trust in yourself and reality: The Zen master Nissim Amon teaches the following mantra: "Life is Beautiful, It's OK to Enjoy, Everything is Alright."

Know when to say "No": When you say "No" to people (and clients) and "No" to opportunities that do not serve you, you open the door to new things you do want to happen. Freedom is significantly related to boundaries.

Recognize of your limitations: This is an important factor to consider in managing your schedule. Turn off your cell phone when you need to concentrate or have some quiet time for yourself. Take breaks when you really need them. Natalie Ben-David, a transformational leader and life coaching trainer, says that one of the quantum leaps in her career occurred when she started to go to sleep early. It's not about being lazy but about a realistic assessment of your capabilities. Even a car cannot run without fuel.

Do not wait for retirement: Hillel the Elder, one of the most important scholars in Jewish history, said around 2,000 years ago: "Don't say, 'When I have leisure time I will study' – perhaps you will never have that leisure." Hillel the Elder walked his own talk: The story goes that he was extremely poor, and earned his living from manual labor. Half of his salary went to the attendant at the house of study where he was learning Jewish scriptures, and half to providing for his family. Once, Hillel could not scrape together the study fee and wasn't let in; therefore he crawled onto the roof to listen to the lesson through the chimney. The scholars in the hall noticed his figure obstructing the light and had him brought down, nearly frozen to death under a blanket of snow. Hillel eventually became the president of the Sanhedrin (the highest religious and political institution of the Jewish world during about the last two centuries BC).

Life is usually so packed with obligations and tasks that it's easy to neglect what fills us with liveliness and vitality. But if we do not make time for what we want, no one else will do that for us. Always, but always, there will be more pressing things to do, and that usually doesn't wane with time. Thompson, Emery and Porras suggest in their book *Success Built to Last* never to put off to old age or retirement that thing that drives you.

Be king of your castle: Examine yourself and ask: Am I enslaved to my goals or do my goals serve me? Do not become a victim of your job, but harness it to your own benefit. Treat your career as another means to improve your well-being. Remember that your career serves you and not the other way around. Breathe. Enjoy.

Do not compromise: If you make a change in your career or start a new business, I hope with all my heart that you are aiming for a career you love. If not, keep looking. When you find it, you will know. Do not settle for an unfulfilling job. Doing what you love will reward you financially and emotionally, and it will only get better with time. Steve Jobs warmly recommended that:

> *Your work is going to fill a large part of your life, and the only way to be truly satisfied is to do what you believe is great work. And the only way to do great work is to love what you do. If you haven't found it yet, keep looking. Don't settle. As with all matters of the heart, you'll know when you find it. And, like any great relationship, it just gets better and better as the years roll on. So keep looking until you find it. Don't settle.*

Wrapping up:
Positive affirmations regarding your career

One way to cultivate self-love is self-nourishment through positive statements. Positive statements (or affirmations) are sentences with positive, optimistic and compassionate messages that aim to cultivate these same qualities within you. Some call it Positive Thinking, a term that I am not so fond of, as it has gained too many negative connotations and interpretations. **Positive statements are not a way to mute negative voices, but a way to encourage the positive**. When one of my cynical friends doubted the power of positive affirmation I gave him an inverted example: "Imagine you are standing in front of a mirror and telling yourself you're ugly, stupid and incompetent. Don't you agree with me that even if you completely believe in yourself, these statements would adversely affect your mood? " He concurred with me. The same thing, but on the contrary, takes place when using positive affirmation.

A nice story I heard illustrates the power and the working mechanism of positive affirmation:

> One evening an old Cherokee told his grandson about a battle that goes on inside people. He said: 'My son, the battle is between two wolves inside us all. It is a terrible fight and it is between two wolves. One is evil; he is anger, envy, sorrow, regret, greed, arrogance, self-pity, guilt, resentment, inferiority, lies, false pride, superiority, and ego.' He continued: 'The other is good; he is joy, peace, love, hope, serenity, humility, kindness, benevolence, empathy, generosity, truth, compassion, and faith. The same fight is going on inside you and inside every other person, too.'
>
> The grandson thought about it for a minute and then asked his grandfather: 'Which wolf will win?'
>
> The old Cherokee simply replied: 'The one you feed.'

Positive statements are nutrition for the "good wolf," that's all. You can use certain statements even if you do not believe in them one hundred percent. It does not matter. Nothing is one hundred percent true anyway. You can recite them even if you have doubts. Just like the story about the wolves; you do not deny the existence of the "evil wolf," but be sure to feed the "good wolf."

Positive statements also encourage creativity, since they harness the tendency of our brain to solve problems. For example, if you look at a Rubik's Cube you will naturally try to find solutions to arrange it by the correct colors. Similarly, a positive affirmation is a kind of challenge, a riddle even, set before the brain. If you consider it long enough, you may come up with creative ideas or new ways to make this statement a reality.

Positive statements can be used in all areas of life. Some claim that repeating a positive statement for 21 days in a row creates change. Try it for yourself. Select about 10 positive statements and repeat them every day for three weeks. Following are some suggestions for positive affirmations related to career. You are welcome to select from them and/or to make up your own positive statements:

1. I am connected to my calling.
2. I am driven by love.
3. I am worthy as I am, and I do not need to do anything to prove it.
4. My capabilities and talents are expressed fully through my work.
5. I deserve to experience satisfaction and meaning in my work.
6. I do what I love to do, and financial prosperity flows easily to me.
7. I am open and ready to receive abundance.
8. My being happy and satisfied benefits my family.
9. My calling promotes the happiness of everyone I come in contact with.
10. I deserve to live a satisfying and pleasurable life.
11. I am free to choose the most satisfying and enjoyable career for me.

Self-Esteem

Self-esteem and career

The job search process can be frustrating and discouraging. A friend of mine once said: "For me, job-hunting is just like the dating scene. You pass from one job interview to the next, evaluated according to strict criteria. Some employers will give you a negative answer, and some do not even bother to call you back. By the time I do find a job, my self-confidence has been completely eroded."

A long period of unemployment can adversely affect your self-image. The same is true if you are in a job in which you feel you are not realizing your full potential. In Western society, we are measured predominantly by our professional achievements, and this also affects how we evaluate ourselves.

Ronnie, a family man who lost his job due to cutbacks, joined one of my career-change groups. He believed that his prolonged unemployment had compromised his status as the father of the family. "My wife ignores my judgment," he said with pain in his voice. "Even regarding decisions affecting the home or children, I feel she no longer trusts me. It also affects my relationship with the kids. I feel that I no longer have a say." A closer look at the full picture of Ronnie's family situation revealed that he was deeply hurt by the layoff. His self-image as a strong provider had been damaged. Ronnie became impassive and dispirited. He lounged on the couch for hours every day watching TV. His wife, who initially had tried to support him, became desperate. It was she who pushed him into joining the group. During the course, Ronnie also worked on taking on responsibility at home again and setting boundaries for the children. Ronnie started to gain back the appreciation and trust of his wife and children, and this also helped him in the process of finding a new job.

If you are just returning to the career-world after years of unemployment or after working in an unsatisfying job, you may feel you are in an inferior position. This might manifest itself in a hesitancy with which you approach potential new workplaces, or the apologetic tone with which you talk with HR representatives. Perhaps, as in Ronnie's case, your insecurity permeates your close personal relationships. You harbor the feeling that you have nothing to offer or give to others.

If this is the way you feel, don't be hard on yourself. Your feelings are natural and normal. We are so used to defining ourselves by our professions and taking pride in our occupational achievements (in any new encounter the second question after "What's your name?" is often "What do you do for living?") that it is only natural that a seeming lack of achievements would pull us down.

There is no doubt that work contributes to happiness and satisfaction and adds meaning in life; many studies support that. However, those times when we are not working or don't have a career to be proud of present a golden opportunity to rediscover our own value and re-establish a sense of self-appreciation that is independent of external accomplishments. We can believe in ourselves even when our exterior is less glamorous. Paradoxically, this is what will grant us the mental strength to build a balanced and stable career.

Positive self-image is one's belief in their own essential goodness, creativity, unique voice and value regardless of what they have achieved or done in their lives. This is a very important point, especially when we are talking about career and calling, because people often feel that they are worthy only if they realize their potential, make money, or advance professionally. If you believe that your self-worth is dependent on success and achievements, perhaps you think that if you don't achieve your goals then you're a loser/no good/not worthy of love. In most cases, these are cultural, societal or familial messages that have been internalized over the course of one's life.

The higher one's self-image is regardless of their accomplishments, the better they cope with setbacks and failures and the less risk-adverse they are (because errors do not seem destructive). Self-confidence is a cycle that feeds itself; people radiate their self-trust and thus make themselves appealing to potential clients or employers, which in turn reinforces one's sense of worth. When our self-esteem is high we expect more of life and of ourselves. Psychotherapist Nathaniel Branden says that self-esteem is the immune system of our consciousness. "A healthy immune system," he claims, "doesn't guarantee you'll never become ill, but it does reduce your susceptibility to illness and can improve your odds for a speedy recovery if you do get sick." When our self-esteem is high, we are freer to choose what we really want and not what others think suits us. We don't need to "prove" anything to anyone.

Do you appreciate yourself?

> " The bud
> stands for all things,
> even for those things that don't flower,
> for everything flowers, from within, of self-blessing;
> though sometimes it is necessary
> to reteach a thing it's loveliness,
> to put a hand on its brow
> of the flower,
> and retell it in words and in touch
> it is lovely
> until it flowers again from within, of self-blessing. "
>
> **(Galway Kinnell)**

We are all beautiful, but we tend to forget it.

Some time ago I watched an interview on CBS Sunday Morning with Chris Martin, the lead singer of the world acclaimed rock band Coldplay, in which he spoke about his relationship with his wife, Hollywood actress Gwyneth Paltrow: "It's a big leap," he said, "from being a loser to going out with an Oscar-winner. It's a giant leap, like winning the lottery. I was happy to make it."

If you didn't know Martin you might gather that he was an English bum who had been fortunate enough to go out with a glamorous Hollywood star in a real-life reenactment of the film *Notting Hill*. But reality was slightly different; Coldplay won international recognition and success with the release of their first album in 2000. Martin met Paltrow in 2002 and they married in 2003. He couldn't be defined as a "loser" at any time during their relationship.

Frankly, Martin seems quite amused during the interview, and perhaps one should not take it too seriously. But still, his choice of the word "loser" reminded me of what many of us pretty much do: belittle ourselves and underestimate our value. Often there is a huge gap between how others perceive us and the way we perceive ourselves, usually for the worse. The writer Natalie Goldberg says: "There seems to be a gap between the greatness we are capable of and the way we see ourselves and, therefore, see our work."

This reminds me of a guy I dated a few years ago. He was successful and wealthy, and held a senior position as the national sales manager of one of the country's largest food companies. He managed to boost the company's sales by hundreds of percent, which positioned him as a rising star in the company's management corps. He was highly appreciated and received a fat salary and extensive benefits that he rightly deserved. He loved "going to the field" as part of his job and visiting supermarkets and food chains to check on the company's sales in various stores. One day when he returned from a field tour he told me about an older man who worked stocking shelves in one of the stores. "That man," he confessed, "always makes me anxious."

I was amazed to hear him say: "I am afraid to end up like this guy. I'm worried that one day people will see me for the big liar I am, throw me out of the office and make me stock merchandise on the shelves from morning to night."

These, I remind you, were the words of a senior manager, highly appraised and successful by all objective measures.

The bad news is that low self-esteem is trouble. It doesn't matter how successful and respected you are. If you are convinced that you are a loser, it would be quite difficult for others to persuade you otherwise.

The good news is that you can learn anew how beautiful you are. You can be self-confident while you build your career brick by brick. It doesn't matter where you came from and what you learned about yourself in the past.

Building a positive self-image; recalling your worth

How should one build a positive self-image? First of all – recall your value. This reminds me of a nice story:

> *A professor held a seminar in a hall filled with 200 people. He began his lecture holding a $100 bill in his hand.*
>
> *He turned to the audience and asked: 'Who wants this $100 bill?'*
>
> *Everyone's hand went up. So he said: 'I will give this bill to one of you this evening, but first, let me do this ...' And he completely crumpled the bill.*
>
> *He asked again: 'Who is still interested in this bill?' The hands went up again.*
>
> *The professor continued: 'And if I do this ...?' He let the bill fall to the floor and stomped on it. Then he held up the dirty wrinkled bill and addressed the students: 'And now, who still wants this $100 bill?'*
>
> *Everyone's hand went up again.*
>
> *The professor looked at the audience and explained: 'No matter what I did you still wanted the bill because it didn't lose its value. This situation reflects our lives. Many times in life we are trodden upon, or thrown to the ground, and feel we have no importance. But we never lose our value. Clean or dirty, degraded or complete, fat or thin, none of this is of importance; none of this takes away our worth.'*

Positive self-image has nothing to do with achievements, appearance, intelligence or capabilities, in the same way that a diamond doesn't lose its value even if it's raw, dirty and buried deep in the dirt.

EXERCISE:
Recognition of what's good about you

The first step in raising self-esteem is to remember all that is good and wonderful about yourself. The purpose of the following exercise is to recall your positive nature, your good heart. This is the basis for self-appreciation.

Sit comfortably and close your eyes, take a few deep breaths and relax. Try to let go of thoughts and preoccupations with daily life.

During the next ten minutes ponder your basic good nature and your qualities. Note characteristics such as: generosity, gentleness, sensitivity, honesty, courage, your way of caring and loving, devotion, commitment, sincerity.

Voices of criticism, judgment and resentment might rise in you. Try to let go of them. If you cannot, that's fine. Criticism is an expression of integrity and a desire to better yourself. Give yourself credit, if only for that.

I recommend doing the exercise at least once a week. This exercise is a great lever to strengthen your self-image.

Additional suggestions:

Consult three friends or family members and ask them to articulate at least 10 good qualities they appreciate about you. This is a very empowering exercise.

Make a list of 10-15 of your most positive character traits. Keep the list somewhere accessible; your wallet is a good place. Go through the list every time you feel depressed or disappointed with yourself.

Self-defeat in career

Nathaniel Branden, in his classic book *The Six Pillars of Self-Esteem*, says that the higher people's self-esteem is, the more they are determined to express themselves and their sense of inner richness. And the lower people's self-esteem is, the more they need to "prove" themselves, or forget themselves by leading an unthinking mechanical life.

Let's review some ways in which low self-esteem may control your career.

Giving up

An extremely talented and clever woman joined one of my career-change groups. She was in her mid-forties, but had never persevered in any one job for a prolonged time. She lived with her parents and was completely unaware of her high capabilities. She was so convinced that she had no chance at succeeding that she could not define even one dream that she would like to fulfill. This woman genuinely believed that she was an utter failure. Her self-esteem was so low that she had given up on her right to dream.

Sometimes we have dreams but we give up on realizing them before even trying. There is no shortage of talented people who hold jobs that are beneath their competence because they don't believe they could make the really big dreams come true. If you are working in a job that does not match your capabilities there is a good chance that you feel wasted and that your work is meaningless and drab. Sadly, you might avoid engaging in activities that are meaningful to you and which you are really good at; it's hard to find time to do what could really move your career forward or make you happy. For example, you like painting, writing or flying model airplanes but you hardly ever get around to it. You want to start a new career but you are too busy with humdrum chores to apply to new workplaces. You tend to underestimate your self-value, and there are always more urgent and important matters to take care of, usually for the benefit of others. There is also a very good chance you harbor feelings of jealousy, criticism or judgment towards successful people, especially if they are successful in the fields you are interested in.

Jealousy is a visible signpost pointing to what you want. For example, some years ago my sister, who is 10 years younger than I am, wrote a book and published it. I was her tough content editor, very strict and critical towards her writing. At one point I realized I was jealous of her achievement and particularly of her courage! Secretly I also wanted to write a book but I didn't dare to do it, while she – my little sister – did it. It was this recognition that motivated me to realize my dream and write this book.

Self-sabotage

Low self-esteem can manifest itself in various creative ways. The little child within who is frightened, rejected and buried deep down inside does not necessarily knock gently on the door and ask for your help. Quite the contrary. It's more probable that the inner child will behave in ways that remind you of a temper tantrum in the middle of a supermarket. The inner child will try to convince you it's a waste of time to try, and that you are really not good enough. For example, low self-esteem can spark a tendency to confront bosses or clients and quit jobs in a storm of anger. Eventually you will believe that you really can't hold a job for long.

Another pattern of self-sabotage is a chronic loss of interest – full of enthusiasm, you start a new job or begin a new qualification course, but after a while you reach the conclusion that "it's not it," embark on something new with refueled enthusiasm, quit that too and so on. Self-sabotage can also manifest itself through a tendency to be late to important meetings and to miss deadlines.

What's common to all the examples above, and to many other situations (which you may have already experienced), is that you have developed ways of failing in order to prove to yourself that you are incapable and that your attempts to succeed are a waste of time and effort.

To fulfill the dream ... of someone else

Joshua, a young man in his mid-twenties, was a self-employed dog trainer. His business was quite successful but he was dissatisfied. "From an early age," he shared, "I was taught at home that an academic degree is nonsense and the most important thing is to acquire a profession and become independent. I was always told that I'm cut out to work with animals and that dog training is a profession that opens up a lot of possibilities. But the truth is that I hate being self-employed. I hate wooing customers. When I have time, what I really love to do is to take classes with the Open University."

Joshua is an example of someone who was taught that there was one thing he's good at. As an adult he chose that profession even though his heart pulled him in more academic and intellectual directions that were looked down upon by his family. He could not believe he was capable of academic achievement, and didn't think he could choose a different life.

Proving yourself

Low self-esteem can elicit a belligerent spirit and a desire to prove to the world that one is capable of success. This is what happened to Dana, who worked for ten years as a leading researcher in a large pharmaceutical company. She came to one of my groups after she had lost interest in her job and began searching for a more fulfilling career direction. She came to realize that the research era in her life had come to an end, and that it was now time to fulfill her old dream of fashion designing. She said:

> *I was a dyslexic child, and I suffered a great deal from teachers calling me stupid and lazy. In my twenties I was busy proving to myself and to anyone who didn't believe in me that I was smart and talented, so I pursued B.A. and M.A. degrees in biology and worked as a researcher. Now, after I have made it, I finally feel I have nothing to prove anymore, and I can do what I really love – design clothes.*

In any case, whether we give in to low self-esteem or struggle to prove our value, we may find ourselves light-years away from what suits us, from what our heart really wants.

But it is never too late to listen to your heart. We can always start over.

OBSERVATION EXERCISE:
Self-defeating patterns

Do you avoid doing what you really love and are talented at (either in your career or your leisure time)?

In which way do you self-defeat: Are you giving up before you even try? Sabotaging yourself? Struggling to prove you are "worthy?" Any other way? Elaborate as much as possible.

Being a good parent to yourself

One of the best ways to foster positive self-image is to become a good parent to yourself. Treat yourself as a loving and empowering parent would treat you. Even if you weren't appreciated in the past, and even if you currently suffer from patterns of giving up, self-defeat or having to prove yourself as described earlier, you can reconnect with what you really want. You can nurture your belief in your own value, in your ability to succeed and the fact that you deserve it!

One of the central practices of meditation in the Buddhist tradition is Metta meditation. The meaning of Metta is unconditional friendliness. It stands for several meditation techniques that are aimed at cultivating positive qualities like joy, love and compassion. When the Buddha spoke of nurturing love he talked about a radical and very specific quality; about the feelings of a mother towards her only child:

> As a mother watches over her child, willing to risk her own
> life to protect her only child, so with a boundless heart should
> one cherish all living beings, suffusing the whole world with
> unobstructed loving kindness.

The Buddha said that unconditional love should be directed first of all at yourself. No one deserves it more than you do.

A while ago I said in one of my groups that I want to be really satisfied with myself as I am. "Are you serious?" one of the participants asked in amazement. "You are willing to accept yourself as you are? You do not want to change anything?"

"Self-sufficiency," I replied, "is truly loving myself as I am, unconditionally. That doesn't contradict self-improvement. On the contrary."

This woman was divorced, with a child. To illustrate my point I asked her: "How do you feel about your daughter? Would you like her to change, or do you love her exactly the way she is? And does that contradict your desire for her to be happy and successful?"

"Okay," she responded thoughtfully. "Now I understand what you mean."

Caring and believing in yourself is the most important ingredient that will turn any commentary and criticism into a lever for growth. Become accustomed to giving yourself positive and empowering feedback in the process of building your career.

Cherish your achievements, and respect the path you travel and not only the result you achieve.

Focus on the positive and what works for you. I discussed this at length in the chapter on happiness.

Letting go of attachments and freedom of choice (unconditional happiness)

Unconditional love is not dependent on anything. Money comes and goes, success comes and goes, but nothing is changed. Love is still there. One of the characteristics of low self-esteem is conditional love. That is, to love and/or appreciate ourselves only under certain terms – only if we are beautiful, successful, established, with a nice family, prestigious, or other criteria. The criterion becomes a condition for happiness. "If … then" sentences are manifestations of this. For example, "If I find a partner, then I'll finally be happy," "If only I become famous, then I'll be worth something," "If I become rich, then I can enjoy life." In Buddhism this is called "attachment," and it is considered the #1 cause of human suffering. Attachment is slavery to our desires and wishes. Our desire to achieve a particular goal controls us so much that nothing else matters.

When we believe in an "if … then" condition we are enslaved to the future (which is not yet existent) and we forget to enjoy the present. Our current lives are missing something, and are miserable and bland compared to the life we'll have one day when we achieve our goal. In a workshop with meditation teacher Christopher Titmuss, he directed us to focus our attention on a painful part of our body. I focused on my knee. After a while he said: "Now listen to the birdsong and the sounds of cars passing in the street, note the air caressing your face. When we focus our attention on one thing it becomes the only thing that exists, but there are always other things. There is always something more."

When people declare that their lives are devoid of worth, and there is only one thing that can fill the vacuum in their lives, it often makes me feel that the one talking through them is that little child who refuses to eat if his parents won't buy him a toy. It's as if they have a hidden belief that if they starve themselves (no happiness in the present), then something good will happen. A supreme power would intervene and grant their wishes. If they hold on to their goal without noticing the "other things" that exist around them, that will help them achieve it.

When people believe that one goal (like money, success or a relationship) is an exclusive condition for happiness, they are often confusing determination and obsession. One example is a friend of mine who studied mechanical engineering. His life dream was to become a mechanical engineer, so he repeatedly said: "If I don't complete my degree, it will be the end of me." My friend sincerely believed that defining the degree as the one-and-only goal of his life was a manifestation of his determination and willpower. Any attempt to help him see that his chosen profession was only one way to express himself (and was by no means what defined him) was to no avail. End of story: my friend graduated successfully but paid a high personal price, experiencing several panic attacks and having to regularly take anti-anxiety medicine.

Letting go of attachments is not giving up on your desires and aspirations. Desires and aspirations are important. Your passion is the fire of your soul, and is a medium for integrating into the fabric of life. Do not give up on your dreams, and do everything in your power to accomplish them. However, the secret is to remember that you are free to live your life the way you want. You do not need to do anything. You do not need to prove anything to anyone. When you are free you can easily express the bounty of your nature – for your own benefit and for the benefit of your surroundings. The paradox is that the more our self-image is independent of external accomplishments, the more we are free to succeed and fulfill ourselves.

A few years ago I read an interview in the newspaper with an Israeli actress who tried her luck in Hollywood – in vain. In that interview she mentioned her desire to succeed, described the frustrating waitressing job, the pursuit of auditions. At the end of the article she summed up her disappointment and said she had decided to return to Israel and give up on the dream of succeeding abroad. A few years later I came across the same actress (named Ayelet Zurer) when she co-starred alongside Tom Hanks in the Hollywood hit *Angels & Demons*. Frankly, I was very surprised. That old interview with Zurer had touched my heart, and I remembered her disappointment and sorrow about relinquishing her dream. I wanted to understand what brought about the change, and what accounted for Zurer ultimately fulfilling her dream. Searching for new information, I found another interview with Zurer in which she described the birth of her first son, and said that being a mother had become the main focus in her life, even larger than the desire to succeed as an actress. It wasn't long after the birth of her child that she began to get parts in Hollywood movies.

The relationship between Zurer's motherhood and her budding success seems to me not to be a coincidence, and it's very relevant to our discussion about self-appreciation; when all our worth is measured by success and when we feel we must succeed to be happy/find meaning/live a significant life, we are actually in self-defeat mode. The internal pressure rises, it takes a toll on our mental peace and it impairs our ability to relax and express our creative attributes that are vital to success. In Zurer's story, as I understand it, the new reality of motherhood put her dream of becoming a Hollywood actress in perspective, peeled away the layers of drama and enabled, so it seems, new ways for her to better fulfill the dream.

This is called "releasing" or "letting go"; that is, doing whatever you can without internal pressure or being obsessed about it. It does not matter how many hours you work each day. Some of the most liberated people work many hours and some work just a few. What matters is the quality of how you do whatever it is you are doing, how much you act on inner freedom or due to feeling pressure .When I set a goal, I remind myself that I want to achieve it, but I neither have to do it nor am I dependent on it. It's not always easy to transition from "have to" to "want to," but there is a lot of freedom in doing so.

Goals, dreams and desires are some of the factors that make us human beings and are significant means to achieving happiness in life. Letting go of attachments does not imply a relinquishment of will, but rather a clear awareness of our freedom of choice, and awareness of all the wonderful sounds that exist within and outside of us at this very moment, even if our knee hurts.

EXERCISE:
Metta meditation (unconditional friendliness)

One way to raise self-esteem and let go of attachments is by fostering unconditional friendliness toward ourselves. The following exercise, based on traditional Buddhist Metta meditation, is designed for this purpose – to remember that we deserve love and good things in life regardless of our accomplishments.

Find a quiet place. Sit comfortably. The meditation can be also practiced lying down, provided that you do not fall asleep.
Recommended time: 15 minutes regularly over a period of several weeks.
Take a few calm and natural breaths and relax your body.
You can put your hand on your heart. Some people find it helpful.

Recite the following phrases in your heart:

May I be safe and protected from internal and external dangers and enmity.
May I be healthy and strong.
May I be peaceful and happy.
May I be free.
May I love and accept myself as I am right now.

Some guidelines for practicing the meditation:

Remember the quality of unconditional friendliness: *Do not practice in order to achieve one or another specific goal, but to learn to love yourself unconditionally. The more you love yourself, the more you will be free to succeed, but there are no shortcuts. Unconditional love is not a manipulation.*

Repeat the phrases gently and softly: *Do not force yourself to believe these sentences. Recite them as if they were a soft hand with which you gently touch a loved one.*

These phrases are a practice of recollection and expression of love: *They are not prayers or wishful thinking. The premise is that all the qualities – peace, security, happiness, health, freedom and love – already exist within us.*

Resistance: *Objections, sadness or self-hatred may arise while repeating these words. Take note of the resistance but continue reciting the phrases. Treat the internal opposing voices like a beloved child that is resisting you. This child may feel sad or angry, but you continue to love, gently and quietly.*

Be patient: *This meditation is about sowing seeds of love. They will germinate in due course. In order to foster unconditional friendliness it's important that you practice every day or several times a week for at least three weeks.*

You do not have to recite all the lines every time: *You can select a phrase or two that you more readily connect to and repeat them only.*

If you find it too difficult to dedicate the phrases to yourself, you can choose a benefactor – someone whom you feel has truly cared for you in your life, a teacher for example. You can also choose a child. The idea is to choose someone to whom your heart opens effortlessly and without conflict (therefore it's not recommended to choose a spouse or close friends). Picture the benefactor and dedicate the above phrases to this person: "May you be safe and protected..." and so forth. This will help you open your heart and you can return to yourself when you are ready.

Building confidence

Professor Randy Pausch told a story in his final lecture, "Really Achieving Your Childhood Dreams," about a friend of his who had been extremely stressed about debts of several thousand dollars that she owed. In order to cope with the stress, she attended a meditation and yoga class every week on her only free evening. Pausch related how one day he went through her bills and figured out that she could cover all her debts within a few months if she worked on the evenings she devoted to meditation classes. "Maybe you should work on Tuesday nights and give up yoga for a while?" he suggested.

Pausch said it was like a revelation to her. She took his advice and worked as a waitress on Tuesday nights. Not long afterwards she had paid all her debts. Then she could go back to yoga and meditation and really relax.

According to Pausch, the disease was the debt and the symptoms were stress and worry. That's why he recommended that friend treat the disease (debt) rather than focusing on curing the symptoms (worry) through meditation practice.

This story presents the eternal question: **Is it more beneficial to invest energy in revising habits and making concrete changes, or rather in altering our perception of the world?** Should we first raise our self-esteem so that our work becomes more productive, or should we focus on practical changes that will then increase our self-esteem?
It's a "chicken and egg" question: Is high self-esteem achieved through an internal change of perceptions or through taking direct external action?

I believe that the truth lies somewhere in the middle. Low self-esteem can make us unconsciously choose courses of action that are rather unproductive, beneath our abilities or that aim at "proving" our value to others. Heightened self-esteem will help us identify and eliminate destructive patterns of self-defeat and will motivate us to choose to realize our potential. However, it is important in this context to talk about fear. Avoiding action is often a product of fear, and dodging a confrontation with what frightens us weakens and undermines self-esteem. One example is a case which my good friend Boris, who is a psychologist, described:

> *After working for a year and a half with a patient regarding his shyness and difficulty in flirting with women, we had reached a point where I told him it was time to go to a bar and start a conversation with the first nice lady he laid eyes on. We had come to the stage where talking about the problem had become another way of stalling and avoiding dealing with the issue.*

Resolute action in itself can be a corrective emotional experience that alters perception of the world and oneself in ways that many hours of reflection and introspection will not.

In her book *I Could Do Anything, If Only I Knew What It Was*, the career counselor Barbara Sher talks about her work with ex-addicts to help them create a new life for themselves. She says that these former addicts had never developed the skills they needed to succeed in the real world, and their self-esteem was low. They saw themselves as no more than "ex-junkies." These people could not afford to wait any longer in building a positive self-image to develop skills and find jobs, so the program's facilitators worked with them in a way they called "acting as if": they instructed the participants to dress as if they respect themselves, to apply to jobs as if they were first-class candidates and to act as if they deserved the job they were going for – even if they did not really feel that way. Sher says that this play-acting succeeded big-time. After a while, the ex-addicts did things they had not believed they could do: they made speeches, worked in teams and formed new relationships. Their self-images soared!

Canfield, Hansen and Hewitt claim in their book *The Power of Focus:*

> *There's no greater way to build confidence than getting things done. Create an environment of accomplishment every week. Focus on your three most important targets. Every day do something that moves you closer to finishing a project, closing*

a sale or expanding a relationship. Don't allow yourself to be distracted or interrupted. By doing so you'll eliminate the feelings of guilt and failure. Take one small step at a time. Make sure these mini goals are realistic ... Accept the fact that you need to lose sometimes before you can win.

I believe that long-term change requires determined and courageous action whilst still paying attention to one's inner world – feelings, perceptions, beliefs, needs, will, motivation and inspiration. Only a combination of the two will bring about the desired change. In this same vein, Stephen Covey, in his book *The 7 Habits of Highly Effective People,* writes about the habit of "Sharpening the Saw." He refers to the analogy of a woodcutter who saws wood for several days and becomes less and less effective, because the sawing dulls the saw's blade. The solution is to sharpen the saw once in a while.

Cutting trees represents all that you do to advance your career, like sending résumés, making presentations, marketing yourself and, of course, doing the actual work. The saw is you. Sharpening the saw is analogous to investing in anything that rekindles your motivation and refuels your creative energy, such as reading inspirational books, participating in a peer group, keeping a journal, meditating, and nurturing close relationships.

As a rule of thumb I recommend reversing the natural tendency. Highly practical and target-oriented people tend to work excessively, and forget to take care of themselves, listen to their feelings, and invest in relationships. In contrast, reflective and introspective people tend to embrace endless training and postpone the moment of "taking the plunge" and implementing what they have learned.

Ask yourself what type of person you are. Are you a doer or an observer? Do you work tirelessly or learn and develop but postpone any application? If you are a doer, continue to be so, but carve out time to learn and recharge your batteries. If you are a perpetual learner, continue to be so, but be sure to regularly apply what you have learned. Do the opposite of your natural inclination. This will ensure your growth and boost your self-esteem.

Self-esteem and criticism

Constructive criticism and lesson-learning are instrumental means of growing and improving. Take, for example, my friend Joel, who participates in an amateur photography group. He decided he won't upload any more photos to the group's Facebook wall. "There is no point," he claimed, "it's either the guys love your photo and give it lots of Likes, or ignore it altogether. Then you should infer that it's no good. They just never write anything useful." In other words, people do not give feedback. In one episode of the series *Seinfeld*, George goes to a job interview with a piece of green salad stuck between his front teeth. The interviewer licks his teeth and makes funny faces so that George might get the hint, but he doesn't. Unfortunately for George, no one tells him straight-out that he has something stuck in his teeth. He didn't get the job.

I would hope that people would let me know if I have something stuck between my teeth, and I assume you would too. Similarly, constructive criticism is very important when we want to assess our conduct in a business meeting, the effectiveness of a document we produced, or the quality of artwork we've created. Criticism can come from within or from outside. When we find that external feedback is lacking, it is extremely important to listen to our inner voice that demands precision, attention to detail and uncompromising quality. Without it, we will find ourselves, in the best case, croaking futilely in *America's Got Talent* auditions, and then be surprised that we appear in the "funny auditions" category on YouTube rather than going to Hollywood. In the worst case, we will invest our precious time and money in a career or business that does not suit us. Constructive self-criticism is a healthy manifestation of positive self-image, self-awareness and realistic self-esteem.

However, the words "constructive criticism" can be misleading. Sometimes the line between constructive feedback and destructive criticism is blurred, and we flog ourselves instead of nurturing our development. Constructive self-feedback and self-awareness are, as mentioned, valuable and important qualities, whereas destructive criticism is an expression of low self-esteem. Demeaning feedback can discourage you, weaken you, and devour your strength while you're building your career, at a time when what you really need is self-belief and the full power of your engines.

Low self-esteem is usually a manifestation of internalized messages you received from your immediate childhood environment, whether it be parents, siblings, teachers or friends. If you were regarded with disrespect, contempt or skepticism about your abilities as you were growing up, the chances are good that those negative messages accompany you in adulthood, and that it is difficult for you to believe in yourself and your abilities.

However, the mere awareness of the origin of low self-esteem is not always enough to activate a change. That's because somewhere inside of you, you still accept the belief that criticism and self-flagellation are beneficial. It's very common; we live in a society that believes in criticism and negative feedback. Jack Kornfield, a renowned American Buddhist teacher, says that in one of his meetings with the Dalai Lama he told the latter that many people in Western society suffer from self-hatred. The response of the Dalai Lama, as depicted by Kornfield, was of disbelief. The concept of self-hatred is apparently far less common in the Far East.

Many people hold a belief (of which they may be unaware) that criticism has the power to spur action and create change, though reality does not support this perception. In fact, the opposite is true. Studies show that people with high self-esteem and belief in themselves and their capabilities lead more successful lives. However, ensnared by the power of our destructive obsession with criticism, many of us disparage ourselves (and others) again and again, all in the hope that our self-flagellation will propel us towards one goal or another that we have set for ourselves.

OBSERVATION EXERCISE:
What do I gain from criticism?

Ask yourself:

How is self-criticism beneficial to me? What do I gain from self-flagellation?

Write down at least 15 responses. Write quickly and without giving much thought to your answers.Write down every thought that occurs to you, no matter how stupid it seems.

Answers could be for example:
*It makes me feel that I'm doing **something** (at least I'm reproaching myself).*
It keeps me small (I am afraid to grow up).
I would rather fight with myself than confront my boss.

What do you learn about your fears and about your needs from what you've written? How can you transform your observations into action? Which positive and constructive measures can you take instead of criticizing yourself?
Examine, for example the statement: "I criticize myself because I am scared of growing up and assuming responsibility." Turn it into: "I intend to dare more. I intend to take responsibility."
Examine the statement: "I criticize myself instead of confronting others." Turn it into: "I have a right to express my feelings and thoughts. I plan to pursue more open and sincere communication."

EXERCISE:
Dealing with the internal critic

If you are repeatedly hard on yourself, severely criticize yourself and generally feel that you are inadequate, you are probably dealing with the "internal critic," a disapproving, discouraging and fearful voice that paralyzes your progress.

Destructive criticism is based on fear. Instead of ignoring it, try to get close to it and figure out what scares you. *Then you can get back to building your career in a much more free and liberated fashion.*

1.   *Take a plain sheet of paper and draw an image of your internal critic.*

This might be a drawing of a person, an animal, a monster or anything else that comes to mind. For example, in one of my groups a man drew the number "1" as a representation of his internal critic. For him, it expressed the perfectionist voice telling him that if he's not the best in his field, then he is no good at all. He felt that this voice blocked his developmental process.

2. Draw balloons around the critic depiction, and fill them in with all the oppressing sentences that the critic is saying to you. For example: "You're a failure!" "You have no idea what you're saying." "You're really not ready for this." "You're dull and mediocre. It's time to admit it."

3. Observe your drawing. Which emotions does it evoke in you? These may be feelings of despair, inferiority, anger and frustration. Also note the sentences you wrote. Try to recall who has said these words to you in the past.

4. Next, write a letter to your internal critic or to the specific persons who discouraged you in the past. Tell them frankly what you think about their attitude and their negative opinions. Honestly vent your feelings about how this affected you and hurt you. There is no need to censor or filter the content of your letter; it is for your eyes only.

EXERCISE:
A dialogue with the internal critic

This is another technique I like to use to tackle the internal critic. The empty chair technique is a commonly used psychodramatic method to open a door to an internal dialogue.

Place two chairs facing each other. One chair represents your critical voice; the other one represents your capable self who wishes to express itself and succeed. Keep a dialogue going between these two voices while you respectively switch between the chairs. Make sure you talk and respond in the correct role depending on which chair you're occupying. That is, if you sit on the internal critic chair, respond and speak on behalf of the critical voice, and if you sit on the chair of your capable self, talk and respond on behalf of your capable self. Conduct a free dialogue while moving from chair to chair.

> *The power of this technique is that it allows you to differentiate between separate voices, and to untie the knot of an inner conflict where ability and criticism mingle. Using this exercise you might be able to identify which fear underlies the criticism, and realize which person from your past had sown the seed of that fear. You also have the opportunity to give full expression to the vulnerability and anger of your capable self which is repeatedly blocked by the critic.*

Knowing how to give constructive criticism

One of the predominant features of low self-esteem is loud, insulting and mean self- criticism. If you've tried (to make a sale, "ace" an interview, create your project, present yourself, etc.) but didn't succeed, self-destructive criticism will not hesitate to hit you on your head, reminding you that you are a loser; you should give up on the big ambitions and stop wasting your time. Destructive self-criticism is a way of trying to keep yourself in a seemingly safe and familiar zone where there is no fear of rejection or failure because you neither take risks nor do you offer any significant contribution.

Let's take a look at the outlines of destructive criticism vs. positive and empowering feedback:

1. **Specificity vs. generalization:** Constructive self-criticism analyzes each case of failure on its own and does not generalize or formulate universal laws. Generalized thoughts like: "I do not interest anyone," "All employers are only looking for younger employees," or "It's impossible to succeed without higher education" are expressions of low self-esteem and oppressive criticism.

Try to examine each case individually. My brother always says: "There are over seven billion people in the world, so it's a sure thing that every rule has at least a few exceptions." In my experience, he's right. A good friend of mine completed her M.B.A. degree and looked for a job as an organizational consultant. Most jobs in this field are full-time and quite demanding, and it's difficult to find work if you don't have several years of practical experience. My friend was a new mother, and she was looking for a part-time job. Miraculously, she found one. The interviewer liked her so much that he hired her despite her having had no experience and wanting to work part-time. She had kept an open mind although the chances of finding such a job had been slim.

If you weren't successful at an interview, don't say: "I'm so bad at interviews," but rather ask yourself, "Why did I fail at this specific interview?" This way you can learn from experience and make amendments in the future. Be specific and localized in your feedback: reference it to specific behaviors, avoid universal laws and examine each case on its own.

2. *Comparison and ideal self-image vs. time to develop:* Another manifestation of destructive criticism is that you measure yourself against those who are much more experienced and prominent than you are: "Who do you think you are – Donald Trump?" "Who are you, Leonardo da Vinci?" Evaluating yourself against extremely high and perhaps unrealistic standards creates tremendous and crippling pressure. Holding on to an "ideal self" creates a similar impact; if you think that less than perfect is worthless, you will constantly experience disappointment, frustration and despair.

Remember that even the most successful people were once at their starting line. They fumbled, made mistakes and have consequently discovered their path. Accept experimentation, uncharted exploration and failures as part of your learning process. Do not give up on your quest for excellence, but accept that you are still a novice at the beginning of your journey, especially if you are embarking on a new career or setting up a business from the ground up. Give yourself time to experiment, make errors and assimilate your experiences. Less than perfect is ... a perfect start!

3. *Correctable vs. "never enough":* Constructive feedback focuses on specific and changeable features of your behavior or your work, for example, your body language in job interviews, your tendency to react without thinking, or incorrectly pricing your products. However, self-flagellation is a manifestation of low self-esteem. Sentences like: "You always destroy sales meetings," "You are hopeless," "Here, you can't be trusted again," "You'll never make it," are examples of self-flagellation. Whatever you do, you feel you are not good enough.

The set of beliefs that you hold about yourself are often a collection of habits and behaviors that you can choose to modify and repair. Refrain from making generalizing, all-inclusive and semi-mystical statements like "It will never work," or "I don't have a chance." These sayings are not descriptions of your situation but rather an expression of low self-esteem.When you fail, define precisely what can be corrected and improved the next time.

4. Recognition of success vs. self-blame: Positive feedback goes hand in hand with recognition of successes and improvements – noticing advancements you make and positive changes you undergo. You cherish your achievements at least as much as you pay attention to what should be repaired. However, devastating criticism tends to ignore improvements – taking the positive as a given – and puts major emphasis on the negative and what is missing.

Appreciate the small steps of progress. Celebrate your successes. At regular intervals, once a month for example, look back and see how you applied lessons learned and managed your career in better ways; whether you market yourself better to new customers or potential employers, or whether you manage your time more efficiently, you've made progress and are more proficient in your line of business. Change for the better is not obvious. The more you cherish your achievements and your learning process, the more motivated you will be and the greater the reinforcement to improve even more.

(And here is my cat cherishing her achievement and showing off the large rat she caught)

5. *Reliance on facts vs. perceptions:* When it comes to decision-making, it's advisable to consider the objective data, facts and options. Low self-esteem might lead to believing that one "feels" or "knows" how others will see them or think of them (negatively of course), so there is no use trying to achieve anything. Take into account all rational considerations in your decision-making process. Intuition does have its time and place, but if you constantly feel that "it won't work," ask yourself whether it is really intuition, or whether it's fear and doubt in disguise.

6. *Dwelling on failure vs. analyzing success:* A successful businessman/woman will not think about how to sabotage a deal, but rather how to close it successfully. On the way to a meeting with a new investor he/she won't murmur to themselves: "Oh gosh, I really blew it last time. What I did was ..." Instead, they will look in the mirror, give themselves a pep talk, straighten their clothes, and try to remember and implement everything they know about being successful. It is important to learn lessons but also to know when to move on and not focus on failures. Natalie Goldberg writes: "I've been in writing workshops where we have worked on a bad poem, criticizing it for twenty minutes. That's ridiculous. It's a waste of time. It's like trying to beat a dead horse into running again." She cites literary critic Mark Van Doren's answer when asked why he didn't review some works in more depth: "Why bother talking about something you don't like?" Learning from success is the way to further succeed.

7. *Self-belief vs. contempt:* Constructive self-feedback, even if it's prickly, always stems from friendliness, appreciation and a belief in your own capabilities. Destructive criticism, however, is dismissive, demeaning and insulting. This is the central and most important feature that distinguishes between positive, constructive feedback and destructive or oppressive criticism. **Positive criticism always includes self-appreciation, self-respect and confidence in your abilities.** One way to ensure that you give yourself a fair and empowering feedback is to keep in mind how someone who really loves you, believes in you and cares about you would treat you. What words would they use? In which tone?

How to face criticism?
Some ideas to think about

Feedback and lesson-learning are necessary and inevitable in the process of building your career. It is important to notice what works for you and what you should improve. Avoiding or discounting others' feedback and constantly patting yourself on the back will arrest your growth. These reactions are expressions of lack of self-awareness and low self-esteem. However, to do some empowering lesson-learning you might want to consider the following ideas:

Beware of those who belittle you: Usually these are people who are low on self- esteem themselves and belittle other people so as to feel better about themselves. Rumi said: "Ignore those that make you fearful and sad, that degrade you back towards disease and death."

Criticism sometimes comes in disguise, like a wolf dressed in sheep's clothing. I remember the first time I worked as a group leader; I was 19 years old, fresh out of high school. Back then I was shy and insecure, and presiding over a group of sassy and opinionated teenage girls was a difficult and confusing experience for me. My father, out of genuine care and love, wanted to help me. I remember how he invited me out one night, it was only him and me, for a conversation in which he said to me: "My dear, everyone needs to know what they can and cannot do. There are many, like you, who are simply not cut out for working with people. You should think about a different direction in life." His words wounded me and intensified my insecurity. Following this unfortunate and influential first experience in group leadership, more than ten years passed before I realized that I did want to work with people and that I was actually pretty good at it.

I know my dad was full of good intentions. He tried to help me and save me from a miscalculated professional choice. But in fact what he did was to project his own insecurity onto me.

Beware the advice of frustrated people with low self-esteem. They usually find it difficult to encourage you and believe in you because of their own difficulty in believing in themselves. This is especially true if you are pursuing a direction that the other person always wanted to pursue but never did. Hilde Domin, a significant post-World War II German poet, said she had always felt that her husband, who was a scholar and intellectual, was envious of her and the fact that she was writing. When she first showed him her poems, he remarked: "Look at what the cat dragged in." Only after his death did she begin to devote herself fully to writing.

In a case closer to home, a participant in one of my groups would constantly give me advice and tips as to how to better lead the group. This is quite a common phenomenon in group dynamics; sometimes people need to confront authority to confirm their own identity. However, in one of the last sessions I suddenly realized the root of her criticism. It turned out she was also a group facilitator, but she did not actually work in the field. I sensed that, in her frustration, she looked at me sideways and seemed to say to herself (and to me): "I could do it better."

Perceived external criticism reflects self-doubt: Messages of doubt and lack of faith that you receive from your environment usually reflect unconscious internal criticism you harbor towards yourself. External criticism that doesn't sync with your beliefs about yourself will not make an impression, just as you would probably dismiss a stupid remark like "the sun shines at night." It will go in one ear and out the other.

If people around you repeatedly criticize you, search inside for points where you do not believe in yourself. Take this as an opportunity to trace your own self-doubts. You might discover that your own lack of confidence draws you to people who doubt you. Perhaps it's time to boost your self-confidence and look for new and more supportive friends.

Finally: don't let criticism stop you

Often it's helpful to simply remember that self-doubt is a natural part of any significant endeavor: criticism, belittling and doubts are manifestations of deep-seated fear of change. For processes of change – and building a career is definitely such a process – require daring and emotional courage. Barbara Sher says: "You do have to take an emotional chance when you let yourself love something." Construction of a new career is a process of nurturing love, towards yourself and towards the world, and it requires faith and courage.

Marianne Williamson has suggested this in her poem (which is often attributed to Nelson Mandela's inaugural address):

> *Our deepest fear is not that we are inadequate.*
> *Our deepest fear is that we are powerful beyond measure.*
> *It is our light not our darkness that most frightens us.*

If your thinking is taking on general and dramatic terms, such as "It will never work," "I stink," "That's terrible," "It is meaningless," "Who the hell do you think you are?" then let it be. Accept it as the voice of the "afraid you," let it continue with its dramatic babbling and proceed with what you do. Your aspirations are important and of significance. It is worth fighting for your passion.

Williamson's poem ends with the following powerful words:

> *And as we let our own light shine,*
> *we unconsciously give other people*
> *permission to do the same.*
> *As we are liberated from our own fear,*
> *Our presence automatically liberates others.*

Trust yourself;
find your personal style for success

You want to succeed. You want to express your own unique voice. Now what?

The natural human desire to succeed has generated extensive and rich literature that attempts to crack the secrets to ultimate success. Trainers, researchers and writers rolled up their sleeves and examined the habits of successful people, successful companies and thriving businesses. If you google the words "tips for success," you will get over half a billion results.

There is no doubt that adopting mentors is hugely important, and learning from those who are successful is valuable and can preclude your making many mistakes. Anthony Robbins, the world-renowned life coach, said that if you want to succeed at something you should learn from those who have already "made it." Learn their belief-system, their habits. Step by step, do what they did, and then you will succeed as well. That's good and important advice. The wheel already exists; there is no point in reinventing it.

However, be careful when acting on this advice. Imitations are boring and uninteresting. Doing what has done before is no guarantee for success. **You need to fill your action with life and soul, which is something that is unique to you. Listen to others and then decide on your own.** Tips and good advice from others cannot replace your instincts, your gut feelings and the road you personally take to success. Automatic acceptance of others' techniques for becoming successful can confuse you and disrupt your attention to your own pace, your own agenda, your priorities and your personal style. Rumi said: "Do not be satisfied with the stories that come before you. Unfold your own myth." There is a famous phrase from the Chinese Zen master Linji: "If you meet the Buddha on the road – kill him!" That is, don't blindly accept authority even if it has been proven as wise as Solomon and has won world acclaim.

Moshe Feiglin, a controversial Israeli politician, described in his debut speech in the 19th Israeli Parliament how he became so determined and loyal to his views, despite their being considered extreme or unusual:

When I was a young platoon commander in a reserve unit, I did my yearly thirty days of security duty and another week or two of training ... I was assigned to one of the posts of the Jordan Valley, a post that overlooks one of the bridges of the Jordan River; a post that has what is called in military jargon a 'porcupine.' In other words, a small mini-post juts out from the post all the way down to the border itself. I decided to position myself, as the platoon commander, at the position that I saw as being the most important. We set about getting organized for active duty.

In the evening, the platoon commander arrived. He was checking on all the different posts that our platoon was guarding. And he asked me: 'Feiglin, what do you say? Is everything all right?'

I said to him: 'No.'

'What is the problem?' he said to me.

I said to him: 'Look, do you see that bridge? There is a hidden path here. Anyone can cross it without anybody noticing him, and he can get over there, under that ridge and go around the post, come from the back and shoot everyone without anybody even noticing.'

To my astonishment, the platoon commander, instead of writing down what I had said and taking care of it, admonished me severely in front of my soldiers, and left the post.

And I – sinned and transgressed – instead of making an issue of it, leaving my post, running to the brigade commander – no matter what – insisting that the problem be taken care of, I said: 'Fine, maybe things that they see from there, we do not see from here. Maybe he knows something that I don't know.'

The reserve duty ended, I returned to my home, to my family, to my business, and after approximately a year, precisely what I had feared – happened [a soldier was killed].

> *The pain that I felt at the moment that I heard what had happened on the news has not left me. I remember it very well. And I decided then, still as a private person who was unknown, that there is no such thing as 'Things that they see from there, we do not see from here.'*
>
> *What I see is the truth, it is the reality. And I will not take 'No' for an answer ... Nobody should tell us stories ... What we believe is in the realm of our authority ... We are responsible to take care of it and promote it.*

Feiglin's story is very dramatic, I know. It deals with questions of life and death. However, I believe that self-fulfillment is quite a dramatic issue too. It can make the difference between a happy and a bitter life. The British businessman and billionaire Sir Richard Branson said: "There is no greater thing you can do with your life and your work than follow your passions – in a way that serves the world and you."

Do not get me wrong; learning your domain is essential – whether it's hard-core professional knowledge or managerial aspects such as business development and marketing strategies. Feeling that "I can do it all by myself" is beginner's arrogance (and, mind you, stupidity). But listening to others only while dismissing your inner voice and insights is a recipe for confusion and lack of authenticity. Instead of driving your business forward you will feel that you are fluttering and shaking with every passing breeze.

Mihaly Csikszentmihalyi highlights in his excellent book *Creativity*, the diversity of successful managers' personal styles, sometimes even to great extremes. He quotes John S. Reed, the former CEO of Citicorp, who says that the CEOs of the 50 most successful companies differ markedly in their dispositions and their management styles, while the only thing common to all is that they are results-oriented:

> *Well, because of my job, I tend to know the guys who run the top fifty, one hundred companies in the country, and there's quite a range ... It's funny, there is a consistency in what people look at in*

business people, but there's no consistency in style and approach,
personality, and so forth. There is not a consistent norm with
regard to anything other than business performance ... There are
guys who drink too much, there are guys who chase girls; there
are guys who are conservative, do none of the above; there are
guys who are very serious and workaholics ... it's quite amazing,
the range of styles. You're paid to run companies, they watch
quite carefully as to results. But there is a lack of consistency on
any other dimension. How you do it seems to be a wide-open
variable.

When I started out as a freelancer I joined the mailing lists of many mentors. My inbox was bloated with advice on how to be successful, tips on business-building strategies and on ways to attract new clients. Aside from my time being consumed by reading all those emails, I felt that all that surplus information confused me and made me feel small and stupid. Furthermore, each mentor emphasized something different which sometimes contradicted the others: for example, one mentor talked about massive action as the key factor for success. Another mentor, just as accomplished, emphasized mainly long-term planning.

I found that the way to find my personal style in building my business is to stop relying on the wisdom and advice of others, and to begin relying on myself. I found that not everyone's approach suits me. Ultimately, each teacher's style largely reflects their personality and not necessarily any absolute truth. For example, task-oriented mentors will give you different advice than people-oriented ones. I belong to those people with more artistic inclinations. Fixed routines that fit like a glove for more organized and calculated people suffocate me. At a certain point I became very choosy about my mentors, about the books I read and advice I follow.

Another key, as I discovered, is to be focused and selective – to listen only to those who address what currently bothers me. And I do this after – not before – I search for answers inside myself. For example, when writing on a specific topic, I always ensure at the very start that I know what I have to say about it; that I have defined my personal statement and my own insights into the subject. Only then do I explore the issue further and check out what has already been said. Listening to others is especially beneficial after you have figured out what you think and feel. Cookie-cutter solutions are a dubious shortcut. It's true with work and it's true with relationships.

This is what works for me.

Check out what works for you.

EXERCISE:
What is your success style?

The following exercise is based on the assumption that how you do anything is how you do everything. That is, there is a common denominator in the ways you deal with different challenges, both large and small.

Think about a project you have completed successfully, something you enjoyed doing and that you're proud of. This could be a professional project; writing an academic paper; creating a work of art; buying or selling a car; building a new house or hosting a birthday party for a multitude of guests.

Identify the terms which enabled your success:

1. *How did you manage your time in terms of dedication to the project and leisure and family time? Did you need to focus on one central goal, or did you easily juggle many different tasks?*

2. *How did you manage uncertainty, doubts and concerns that arose along the way? What helped you get over them?*

3. *Did you seek the help of certain people? Who were they? In which ways did they assist you?*

4. *Did you have to report to someone on the results of the project? Did you have to work under financial or time-pressure? Did external pressure help or inhibit you and how?*

5. *Under which conditions did your creativity flourish? What helped you solve problems that arose along the way? What promoted your coming*

up with new ideas? Are you more creative when you have absolute freedom or when you are subject to external definitions to your work (like academic guidelines, a presentation which subject was dictated, etc.)?

Additional questions:

1. Do you work better in the morning? At night?

2. Are you capable of shutting out all else and focusing on the subject at hand over short periods of time or do you have concentration difficulties and you need to assign yourself longer working periods? If it's difficult for you to muster concentration, maybe scheduling less than a one-hour work period is a waste of time.

3. After how much time of continuous work do you "lose it?" How often do you need to take a break?

4. Do you plan doing tasks in terms of days? Or in terms of hours?

Make a list of all the factors that helped you succeed in managing the project. Make a list of factors that stalled you, and which you would like to change in the future.

From these two lists, derive your key to success.

If, for example, you work best when you have someone to report to, set a weekly meeting with a friend or colleague and report to him/her about your progress. Alternatively, find a personal coach, set goals and objectives together and report to him/her at fixed intervals. Collaborate with colleagues. Your commitment to them will push you to work.

Identify your habits that generate success and stick to them. If you are particularly alert in the morning, then get up early. Stay resolved. However, remember that the rules you set serve you and not vice versa. For example, I noticed that the best way for me to deal with the burden of unpleasant tasks is to do them first thing in the morning, and then have my mind clear for the more enjoyable stuff. However, after a while I noticed that it's hard for me to get up in the morning, so I decided to dedicate the first two hours of my day to one of my favorite things – writing – as motivation to get out of bed, and then move on to other tasks. I played with it.

Spread your unique light – or, what do you have to offer?

" *Every person needs to know and understand*
That inside him there is a candle lit.
None is like any other
And there is no one without a candle.
Each person needs to know that he must strive for all
to discover his candlelight,
Kindle a great bonfire with it
And light the whole world. *"*

(Rabbi Kook)

Fostering high self-esteem is a process of recollection. We are unique and creative, but we tend to forget that. We are strong, but we have learned to turn our back on our strength, or use it for self-defeat. Rabbi Kook's poem argues that everyone has their own unique value. Whatever you can give, no one else can – because your unique contribution is constituted of your personality, your life experience, your knowledge, and the innumerable life circumstances that are special to you.

As a part of your journey to realize the career of your dreams, it is important to clearly and precisely define your unique value as an employee and a service provider: how you and your products can benefit others; what potential clients or employers gain from engaging with you. The better you define to yourself and to others what you offer, the more your confidence will grow and you will market yourself much better.

So what makes you a wonderful professional?

In other words, **what do you offer?**

You'll be surprised to know how many people have trouble answering this question. They apologize, or use long sentences or vague words that do not say much. For example, a parents' group facilitator defined her workshops as "unique and different workshops that will help you create a better relationship with your children." What does that mean? "Unique" and "different" in what ways? It's all too vague and generic. **Be specific.** It is imperative that your clients understand exactly why they should work with you, and whether you can meet their needs.

Another thing, no less important, is that the better you define what you offer and what you want in return the more likely you will be to attract those clients who are most desirable for you, and not waste time on people or jobs that are unpleasant, don't pay, and that you don't want to work with.

How to answer the question: What do I offer?

1. Your products: Define your products in terms of **benefits** rather than features. That is, point to what your clients will gain and not only to "dry" product features. Look at the example of how large companies advertise their products. Fashion companies offer clothes (product), yet they market convenience, being up-to-date, elegance, coolness (benefits). Airlines offer flights (product), but they market adventure and enjoyment of life (benefits).

One key in referring to benefits is to create an appeal to emotions. Use terms that move your clients, inspire them or give them confidence.You might best describe examples of your past successes and how your knowledge, skills and talents in previous projects or jobs contributed to your clients' satisfaction.

2. Remember that a part of the product is you, ***who you are as a person.*** Presently, there is a huge range of businesses in every domain, and many other people compete with you for any given position. One of the significant things that customers and employers are looking for is people with high integrity, motivation and dedication. In short, they look for people they can rely on.

When you talk about what you offer, also mention your positive personal qualities that make it rewarding to work with you, for example: motivation, diligence, creative problem-solving, dedication, determination, leadership skills and so forth. Every domain requires some different qualities. For instance, in the field of therapy, empathy and listening skills are highly important, whereas in computer programming, problem-solving skills are required. Try to focus on those features that make you outstanding in your specific professional field.

Here too, refer to client benefits, that is, what value they will gain from working with you. For example: "I really believe in my clients," said Shirley, a fitness trainer and dietician. "I believe that every person, at any age, can improve their health significantly. My belief in my clients helps them believe in themselves."

3. Motivation is a point I particularly want to emphasize. People want to work with people who want to work with them. If you are interested in working with a particular client or employer – say it loud and clear! They will take it as a compliment and applaud your motivation.

Groucho Marx's famous registration joke: "I just don't want to belong to any club that will accept me as a member," does not apply to the business world. In my experience in human resources we often recruited inexperienced salespeople who convinced us that they were extremely interested in working for the organization and that they were highly motivated to learn and succeed. Businesspeople actually look for people who are eager to work with them.

In order to connect to your own motivations, do some soul-searching every once in a while, and remind yourself why you do what you do. Recall the love and passion that lie behind your work. Your motivations might be curiosity, love of challenge, or a desire to create, to give to others, to guide people to great results or to improve others' well-being. Your passion is the fire that feeds your work. Live this fire and you will radiate it.

4. Be real: People sense fake. It does not mean you should spell out your weaknesses or your problems, but it does mean being natural, honest and even also sharing your feelings (while maintaining a positive atmosphere, motivation and belief in yourself). Humor, for example, can be an excellent ice-breaker.

In one of my first job interviews, sometime in my early twenties, I was in the running for a secretarial position in a big consulting company. It so happened that I had very little sleep the night before the interview, so I was exhausted and drowsy. I have no recollection of what I said in that interview. I only remember that I was intoxicated with fatigue, which always makes me more talkative and lose control of my tongue somewhat. I got the job.

A few months later I stumbled upon the personnel files of the company's employees and could not resist the temptation to open my own file. The interviewer's report read: "I loved her very very much. I highly recommend hiring her."

I definitely do not recommend arriving exhausted to job interviews, but sincerity and genuineness can help.

EXERCISE:
What do I have to offer prospective clients and employees?

1. *How can you benefit your clients or future employers? How can your work answer other people's needs? Think about your experience, knowledge, skills and talents and translate them into potential benefits for prospective clients or workplaces.*

2. *What is it about your attitude or your personality that makes you an excellent professional?*

3. *What is it that motivates you to do what you do?* **What's the WHY behind your career choice?**

Grief & Loss

Loss and grief and their effect on career choice

Jasmine, a kindergarten teacher for the past twenty years, came to a career-change workshop because, as she said, "I'm tired of being a teacher." Investigation of Jasmine's professional dreams revealed a slightly different picture: in the past few years, Jasmine could not find a tenured kindergarten teaching position, and so she was continually moving from one job to the next. The recurrent parting from the children she loved and from the staff with whom she worked was emotionally exhausting and caused her burning pain. The impetus for Jasmine's wish to make a career change was not because she disliked being a teacher, but because she could not bear any more breakups. She thought she could find a little peace of mind in a different occupation, even if it was less satisfying professionally.

Further along in the process a much deeper pain surfaced: a few years earlier Jasmine had lost a child to a severe illness. The pain of loss endured years after the child's death, and Jasmine had also suffered from severe feelings of guilt. Like many people who have lost someone close to them, and even more so because the loss was a child, she had thoughts such as: "Maybe I did not do enough ... If I had gone to other doctors maybe the child would have recovered." She was also burdened by a guilt that her genetic heritage had contributed to the disease erupting in the child. In any case, it appeared that Jasmine still carried a heavy burden of pain and guilt, and in her professional life she repeatedly reproduced the experience of setting herself up for attachment to children and then painfully losing them.

Stories like Jasmine's are more common than you might think. In her case, the parallel between the initial loss and her professional life is striking. But even when the connection is less obvious, sometimes the struggle to succeed or to open a new door is the result of an old door that wasn't properly closed.

Unprocessed grief, especially if accompanied by feelings of guilt, can be the stick in the wheels of your success. Sorrow, guilt and remorse can establish a strict internal self-punishment reaction, and a very strong belief that "I don't deserve to succeed."

Feelings of grief can also arise after significant separations, and even from the loss of a beloved pet, especially if this occurred in early childhood. A few years ago I met Charlie, a young and talented man, who could not hold on to a job for any longer period of time. It seemed that his difficulty to commit also permeated his personal life; he could not manage long-term relationships and always found a reason to bail on relationships just when they were becoming closer and more intimate. During the counseling process, Charlie remembered a dog his parents gave him after they moved apartments when he was a child. The transition had been difficult for Charlie. He was lonely and could not fit in with his new peers. The dog was a source of consolation during the difficult separation from the school, friends and neighbors he had known and loved, and it became his best friend and confidant. A few months after the adoption of the dog, it ran outside into the street and was killed by a car. It was probably Charlie who had forgotten to close the house door.

The combination of being uprooted from his loved and familiar surroundings, and then shortly thereafter losing the dog had a destructive impact on Charlie. He developed a hidden conviction that anything significant could not last for long, and he subconsciously believed he was flawed and not worthy of enjoying a close and loving relationship. During our meetings, Charlie connected, for the first time in his life, to his deep sorrow over the separation from his old neighborhood and friends, and to the loss of the dog, and the sense of guilt he had harbored through all the years. Expressing and processing those feelings finally enabled Charlie to think seriously about finding a career which appealed to him and to which he was willing to commit. Some time after the process, Charlie also met a woman who has since become his wife.

Like Charlie, **people who experienced many separations, deaths and relocations during their childhood may have developed a belief that nothing of value can last over time.** Perhaps they lose their desire to invest effort and time in doing something significant. Furthermore, those who suffered from emotional, physical or sexual abuse in their past may feel a lack of meaning and experience sorrow over the loss of their childhood and innocence. Intense and unprocessed pain over one's past losses casts a heavy shadow on the present. Professional achievements (or close interpersonal relationships) can give rise to internal anxiety over an imminent loss and fear of a painful fall. In such cases, a general pattern might emerge: fear of success, avoidance of life, evasion of intimate relationships, and difficulty in setting down roots or building anything significant for the long term.

Grief can arise from realizing we have missed opportunities in our professional lives, and from knowing what we can no longer achieve. We may experience sorrow and pain over bad career choices or missed opportunities in our younger years. For example, perhaps during your later career-development, you may feel that had you made a career change ten years ago, you might be in a completely different place today, and would not be suffering rejection due to your age.

If you harbor feelings of sorrow over losses and missed opportunities that are long gone, it is important to acknowledge these difficult emotions, clear them from the table and move forward with a lighter heart. Feelings of grief and loss are very painful, so it's tempting to avoid them, "pull yourself together" and only look forward. But, as illustrated in the examples above, the price of denying the pain is a loss of connection with yourself, and you may constantly find yourself in events in which you reenact the painful experience without knowing why. In addition, a loving and intimate relationship with yourself is a prerequisite for growth in all areas, including professionally. The expression of feelings of grief cannot hurt you, but denial of these feelings surely can.

Processing grief: closing one door and opening another

In dealing with losses and missed opportunities, you may experience feelings of loneliness, grief, guilt and anger, and it might take some time until you finally feel your mind has been eased.

During the process of changing my career I attended a dynamic group with other women who, like me, wanted to switch their occupation. At that time I broke up with my boyfriend and also left my therapist. The group facilitator argued that my pattern of repeated separations was a result of unprocessed separations I'd undergone in the past. I took time to reflect on her words, and at some point I recollected my family's immigration to Israel from the United States when I was around six years old. I'd always felt longing for the land of my childhood, and a little bit out of place in my new country. In my early twenties I went back for a visit. When the plane landed at JFK Airport I almost threw myself on the ground crying, like the pilgrims who come to the Holy Land. I was so excited and felt I had returned home. However, as a child and teenager I never felt the full emotional weight of the immigration. It was through later group work that I realized that I had symptoms of very deep pain over the migration and separation from my childhood friends and the culture and language that I loved. I discovered in myself a deep pool of sorrow, pain and abandonment resulting from this transition.

One of the women in the group, who went through a similar experience when she was little, told me that in the year after the migration she would cry in bed every night before going to sleep. I did not do anything like this. I was taught to be a "tough" and "strong" girl, but the sorrow remained buried inside.

Grief has the effect of sea waves washing over you, making you feel that if you let go, you'll drown; but in reality, feelings of sorrow and grief come and go and pass away. Today I feel I belong to the place where I live, and that although the United States is the land of my childhood, it is no longer the place that I call home. While expressing my grief, longing, and mourning over long-gone childhood memories, I found my commitment to my new chosen profession – group facilitating – developing. I felt a growing need to give to other people, and a desire to plant roots, not only geographically, but also professionally.

Alongside grief, you might experience anger. You might be angry with yourself, about choices you have made, or angry with parents who were not available to fulfill your needs. You also might feel angry with the world, or even angry with the people you lost. Often, grief comes with feelings of guilt that you were not strong enough, brave enough or smart enough. However, as I learned from the process I went through, feelings of guilt are an **illusion of control.** Recognition of our helplessness in the face of life's events is so discouraging that we choose to believe that things could have been different if only we were smarter, stronger or better. But this is an illusion. The truth is that we all do the best we can at any given moment, as you've done at every stage of your life. Practicing empathy, compassion and forgiveness for yourself is the best way to unload the double burden of loss/missed opportunity and the ensuing self-flagellation.

If you feel overwhelmed by pain stemming from loneliness, sorrow and anger, do not stay alone! Share your feelings with a friend or a close family member, or join a support group with people who went through similar losses. See a therapist or a psychologist if you need help to process your emotions. In my case I found solace in conversations with other immigrants who understood my pain.

The following exercise can give vent to emotions as they arise during mourning.

EXERCISE:
WRITING A LETTER TO THE ONES YOU LOST

Write a letter to the person (or pet) you lost. Or you may choose to write a letter to the child you once were.
Express freely whatever comes to mind.

You may feel flooded with immense longings, guilt about things you said or did, or didn't say or do. Maybe you feel angry with the person who died or walked away and abandoned you, or you feel anger at those who hurt you. Everything you're feeling is natural and normal.

*Also, allow room for love and compassion towards yourself. Do not stop before you get to love. **It is very important to forgive yourself for your helplessness and to let go of guilt.***

Repeat the process of writing a letter every time you feel it necessary. Releasing anger, grief and guilt can help you let go of the burden of the past, and to return to live in your full capacity of strength.

Loss as a lever for growth and finding meaning

Loss can also be a powerful lever for the construction of a meaningful life. Professor Mooli Lahad, a psychologist and an internationally renowned expert in coping with trauma and crisis, said in an interview to the business newspaper *Globes*:

> *When a disaster strikes, sometimes all at once daily issues cease to matter. There is no desire to confront reality with its hard meaning and to face the day. The feeling is of impotence and helplessness, and also self-punishment, for the disaster that happened.*

In other words, loss may lead to feelings of meaninglessness, depression and despair. However, Lahad stresses that:

> *Disaster can also be a source of change and growth. Disaster can open the possibility for the bereaved to ask themselves if this is not an opportunity to make a change, to change careers and to embark on a new path that will bring interest and meaning into one's life.*

The Community Stress Prevention Center (CSPC), established by Professor Lahad, has helped in many global crises like the 9/11 attacks in the United States, the tsunami in Thailand and Sri Lanka, and the disastrous earthquakes in Haiti and Japan. Tragically, Lahad has also experienced painful loss in his personal life: ten years after he lost his wife to a fatal disease, one of his sons died from a snakebite during a trip to South America.

Loss can be very painful, and is certainly not a life event one might choose to experience in the first place, but it is possible to choose to grow and learn from the crisis. Sometimes the very recognition of life's fragility raises a strong awareness that life is short and that every moment is precious. This is the view of Yonit Werber, a personal and business-success coach, and an international expert in creating and maintaining high motivation. Yonit's husband died in a work accident a year and a half after their marriage, just two days after her twenty-fifth birthday. Yonit recounts:

> *For me it was a shock that a man of twenty-eight and a half was dead, and it was a shock that anyone could die at any moment. Intellectually we are aware of it, but when it happens to you it's like a bomb. For me it was also enlightening. I realized that life can end any day and therefore we need to make the most of it and enjoy it. I started asking existential questions like: Why have we come into this world? If someone had died, what had been their calling, and what is my calling? If my time on earth is limited, then what do I really want to do with it – irrespective*

> *of what is customary and what's acceptable and what makes*
> *money?*

Yonit decided to switch from working with computers to art therapy, and later to being a personal and business-success coach. On her latest career choice she says:

> *Realizing that in a minute I may no longer be here made me very*
> *passionate about making the time that I am here meaningful.*
> *And by 'meaningful' I mean for myself first of all, and then for*
> *others. There's a reason why I work with people. It's because their*
> *time is limited too, and if I can help them turn their time here on*
> *earth into a life of passion and pleasure, then this is my calling.*

The void created by loss or crisis sometimes forces us to adopt a totally different view of ourselves and the world. This can take us to new places altogether, which, had it not been for the crisis, we might have not reached. For example, several years ago I met a young man named Nathan who had been diagnosed with colitis, a chronic and acute inflammation of the intestine. Due to his medical condition he was required to make a drastic change in his diet, one that included, upon his doctor's advice, switching to easily digestible foods and avoiding everything containing fiber, i.e. fruits and vegetables. But Nathan refused to surrender to the decree to give up everything that he thought was healthy and sensible to eat. He turned to raw food nutrition, and lived on a diet of only fresh fruits and vegetables. Within six months of the transition to the new diet all the colitis symptoms were gone, and the doctors sheepishly admitted that Nathan was clinically healthy. He reports that, since his dietary change, his energy levels, alertness and stamina have increased dramatically, and that he hasn't been sick at all, not even with a runny nose. Nathan believes that had he not had the colitis, he would never have reached such levels of health and vitality. Nathan's illness forced him to commit to his health in a way that most healthy people never do.

Several years ago I went through a crisis that gave rise to strong feelings of helplessness. The emotional and spiritual tools that I had back then to deal with crisis were not sufficient to cope with the situation, and I found myself crying for days on end and suffering greatly. However, the unrelenting pain forced me to find new tools to deal with the situation, and I came out of the crisis a completely different person. The crisis led me to leave behind my perception that everything is up to me, that I am solely responsible for my life, into a consciousness of interdependence – that we are all part of a huge fabric, and there are forces larger than any of us which can guide us out of difficult situations and help us reach unimagined new realms. I had to reinvent myself in the face of a gaping void in my life, drawing from a new attitude towards life and fresh perceptions that changed my existence from the ground up.

Life crises are sometimes the way in which our dreams come true in the most accurate way, even if they come packaged completely differently from how we wish. It's like the story of the man who asked God for a flower and a butterfly and received, much to his disappointment, a cactus and a worm. After a while, when the cactus grew flowers, and the worm became a butterfly, the man realized his wish had been fulfilled.

Such is the case of Amy Purdy, whose story I related in the Happiness chapter. She went through a period of severe loss and rehabilitation after losing both her kidneys, the hearing in her left ear, her spleen and both legs from the knees down as a result of a severe blood infection. Amy tells her life story in an inspiring talk given on TEDxOrangeCoast. She tells how her dream as a child was to be free, to engage in snowboarding and live a life full of adventure and stories – and that her life dream crashed in one moment. But, she recounts, the harsh physical disability and the loss of the "old Amy" helped her discover the power of imagination and to believe in the impossible. She returned to snowboarding and won three back-to-back World Cup gold medals in adaptive snowboarding! In addition, she co-founded a nonprofit organization called "Adaptive Action Sports" for young people with physical disabilities who want to engage in action sports (This organization has since become one of the top snowboarding entities in the United States.).

One of the most amazing things Amy says it that she would not want to change her situation. According to her, her legs did not disable her, but rather enabled her, forcing her to rely on the power of her imagination, and to believe in unseen possibilities. She says that her growth was made possible by limits, that she learned that "a border is where the actual ends, but also where the imagination and the story begin." In other words, she found freedom on a much larger and broader scale than what she had dreamed as a child.

Sometimes a crisis is like being thrown into an abyss. We must grow wings so as not to crash, and those wings will take us to new places we have never even thought possible.

EXERCISE:
Writing a fairy tale

The following exercise is designed to utilize your creative resources and humor to promote growth from crises. The use of imagination and art is a powerful tool in breaking down boundaries of what we think is possible and moving towards the unknown horizon.

This exercise can inspire you in your process of changing careers, and you can use it in time of crisis as well.

Write a "fairy tale" that begins just before you decided to change your career, continues with the change process you are now going through, and ends with the fulfillment of your professional dreams.

Use images from children's fairy tales such as: "Once there was a princess/ animal/plant/chick" or anything that describes you. Obstacles can be mountains/castles/forests/lakes/monsters/chases. The happy ending can be conquering the kingdom/dragon-riding/walking to the horizon/gathering around an Indian campfire with your tribe.
These are only suggestions, of course. Go where your imagination takes you.

There is only one condition: *the story must have a good ending, one in which you reach your destination.*

Writing can help you see additional perspectives of your process, as well as creative solutions to difficulties you are facing. This exercise is very moving. If you have someone close to you whom you trust and can rely on, it can be empowering to share your story with them. It might also bring you closer to them.

Happiness

How can happiness benefit your career?

Do you enjoy your work? Do you think that work and pleasure go together? Contradict each other? It turns out that being happy is both fun and lucrative. Philip Green, a British businessman and CEO of Arcadia Group said: "You've got to love what you do to really make things happen." **Studies have found direct links between enjoyment in the workplace and creativity, high energy, motivation and positive teamwork.** These studies also showed connections between enjoyment at work and fast learning, easy recovery from mistakes and failures, higher customer satisfaction, and even reduced illness and workplace absenteeism.

Jessica Pryce-Jones, Founder and CEO of the leadership development organization iOpener and author of *Happiness at Work – Maximizing Your Psychological Capital for Success,* defines happiness as "a mindset which allows you to maximize performance and achieve your potential." One of the myths that Pryce-Jones refutes in her book is that, in order to succeed, companies should focus on their financial capital. According to Pryce-Jones, financial capital can only be achieved if a company functions well – a condition dependent on employees' ability to perform their jobs in the best way.

Pryce-Jones and her team did a comprehensive survey of more than 3,000 employees worldwide and found that the happiest workers were 47% more effective in utilizing their time compared to those who were least happy.

Joy is also sexy. People who are happy, positive and optimistic are more attractive, not only in personal relationships, but also with customers, suppliers and employees. Gretchen Rubin of *The Happiness Project* states that emotions are contagious. People can radiate joy, sadness or energy to the people around them. Therefore, happy workers boost the mood of their colleagues and people feel better working with them. Furthermore, various studies show that happy people climb the organizational ladder twice as fast as those who don't regard themselves as happy. It does make sense that people love having others around them who are positive, motivated and energetic.

In short, nurturing your happiness will definitely benefit you, improve your mood and increase your odds of building a satisfying and significant career. Joy and pleasure are not one of life's luxuries; they provide the space where your creativity blossoms.

The good news is that you can cultivate joy.

What is the more effective way to improve outcomes – focusing on what is working or on what needs to be improved?

People naturally tend to focus on what is missing, inadequate and needs improvement.

Did you, for example, listen to the news today?

If so, you know what I mean.

Want another example? Look at the next drawing. Where do your eyes go?

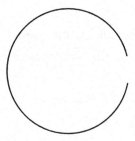

Was the first thing you noticed the missing section in the circle? It is for most people – they focus on the negative, on what is missing. The tendency to focus on the negative is deeply engrained in us. It's possible that it has evolutionary roots. Perhaps humans' need to be on guard against predators and potential attacks reinforced the inclination to be alert, cautious, and to always keep one eye open. Our survival anxiety has strengthened our ability to identify hazards and to perceive what is wrong and needs to be amended. I guess that's at least partially the reason.

However, **many studies show that it's advantageous to focus on the positive, on what's successful and works for us.** Professor Martin Seligman, the founder of positive psychology, showed in various research projects that attention to positive experiences creates a change in the brain, and even wires it differently, in a more optimistic direction. Professor Avi Kluger, a specialist in organizational behavior, has devoted over twenty years of research to examining the impact of traditional employee evaluations (which focus on aspects of work that require improvement) on employees' performance. In recent years he made a 180 degree turn-around and began to investigate the effect of appreciative inquiry on performance.

"Appreciative inquiry" is an organizational development method introduced in the 1990s. It focuses on emphasizing positive aspects of an organization as a way to empower employees and encourage methods that work and yield successes. According to Kluger's findings, organizations benefit much more when applying appreciative inquiry than the traditionally used alternative of critical feedback.

Kluger developed a questionnaire that aims to highlight the positive experiences of the employees in the organization – what turns them on and what makes them happy in their work. The principle is quite simple, yet powerful. Straightforward questions re-direct thoughts to what works, and add energy and vitality: What were your moments of happiness at work today? What filled you with energy? Regarded on the most practical level: identifying and understanding the sources of happiness at work allows them to be replicated over and over again. This is also a wonderful way to increase motivation.

I had a chance to experience the quite dramatic effect of positive feedback when I took voice lessons. Over the course of two years I studied with two different teachers, making little progress. I figured that vocal progress was like that – slow. So it went until I found my third teacher, and for the first time I could finally sing. The difference between my third teacher and the previous ones was that she almost never told me what I did wrong, but focused exclusively on what to do and what I'd done right already. That is, whereas the first teachers corrected me if I made a mistake (focused on the negative), she chose to focus only on the positive. Say, for example, I sang with a closed mouth. She didn't say: "Your mouth is closed," but rather signaled to me to open my mouth. When I did open my mouth she encouraged me with a smile, an approving glance or with words. This is the way she taught me how to breathe correctly, how to control my muscles and also about rhythm and melody. Over a relatively short period of time, the spectrum of my voice expanded by a full octave! And this, as mentioned before, was basically without ever referring back to my mistakes, instead reinforcing what I did right.

To conclude, employees' performance can be improved significantly through appreciative inquiry and positive feedback. It's a relatively simple way in which you can also improve your own performance. If you are searching for a job the principle remains the same: identifying your moments of success and conditions for success, as well as what it is that brings you pleasure, satisfaction and happiness, will allow you to duplicate successes, and, in the process, increase your energy level and motivation.

EXERCISE:
What works for me?
My moments of happiness and success

This is an excellent exercise with which to end and review your day. Do it at least once or twice a week, and even daily during difficult periods. Work with the following questions:

1. *What filled me with energy today? What were my happy moments during work today or in respect to my career?*

2. *Which successes did I experience during the day? These can be small successes like writing a document, having an effective interaction or experiencing a burst of creativity; or larger successes like meeting a deadline, resolving a crisis or finalizing a successful purchase.*

3. *What were the conditions that enabled those moments of pleasure and success? Address this question in terms of external conditions (e.g. location, other people, timetables, challenges,) and internal conditions (your behavior, your attitude and your own qualities, such as determination, diligence, creativity, patience, love, order, humor, etc.).*

4. *What can I do to create more of these moments of success and pleasure?*

Write down your answers to reinforce their significance, and so that you can see your development over time.

Visioning: What do you want to be?

 If you can imagine it, you can achieve it.
If you can dream it, you can become it.

(William Arthur Ward)

Another great way to focus on and nurture the positive is … to create it! Even if you are still in the process of building your business or searching for that next job, you can help yourself reach your desired destination by creating a clear mental picture of the future.

Alex, an author of children's books, tells how imagining his future success gave him strength, energy and the motivation to write:

> *I do not know how I came up with the idea; it's not that I ever went to a course or read a book about guided imagery. But, intuitively, I would imagine at night before going to sleep, and sometimes during the day, how my book would succeed. In my mind I saw it displayed in bookstore windows. I imagined myself reading it to children at public appearances. I even wrote myself a thank-you letter from a hypothetical child who had read the book and wrote to me about how much he enjoyed it and learned from it. This gave me strength and the motivation to write, and to overcome all obstacles until the book was finally published.*

Our self-schema – which is the way we see ourselves – is a living and dynamic system that determines the information we take in and shapes our memories, our emotions and our responses. That is, self-schema is also the lens through which we view the world. If, for example, we expect to fail, then we are more susceptible to absorption of bleak information from the environment. If we expect to succeed, we will be sensitive to uplifting information. We tend to take in information that supports our self-image.

Moreover, people's various mental "glasses" will cause them to interpret the same event in completely different ways. For example, there is a joke about two entrepreneurs – one a pessimist and the other an optimist – who were given the opportunity to sell shoes in a remote place in Africa. "No way," says the pessimist, "they all go barefoot!" The optimist, on the other hand, cries: "It's a market with infinite potential – because they all go barefoot!"

The psychologists Hazel Markus & Paula Nurius developed the concept of "possible selves," that has been used since by psychologists, social workers and organizational consultants with career-development groups. Their model offers alternative ways to see yourself in the future: there is the "expected self," which is the most realistic, sensible and realistic scenario of your life. The "feared self" is the most threatening and dreadful scenario of your life. You are scared by the possibility, and maybe even hardly dare to admit it to yourself or to others. And finally, the "hoped-for self" represents your potential that you wish to realize, though you maybe doubt you will.

The mental picture of our future-self – just like our self-schema – is a living and dynamic system. It is charged with thoughts, feelings, values and goals. People tend to perceive and interpret external information in accordance with the future-self they identify with. This is why creating a vision and a mental picture of the desired future is so important. Markus and Nurius argue that it's not sufficient to have a general desire for the future to be good and promising, but that it is important to give this desire a shape and form, to "dress it up" with concrete images and scenarios of success and happiness. Similarly, the comedian Lily Tomlin once said: "I always wanted to be somebody, but now I realize I should have been more specific."

The mental picture of a positive future-self is an anchor to hold on to and it also increases our motivation to take action. It encourages our creativity to come up with new strategies and plans of action. Ruvolo & Markus undertook a clinical research in which they examined the link between future self-image and success in a given task. They found that the group of subjects that had a successful mental picture of themselves performed the task better, compared with the group that pictured an unsuccessful future-self.

One of the most important things in regard to hoped-for self is to fill it with emotion. The word "emotion" derives from the French word *émouvoir* meaning "to excite" and from the Latin *emovere* meaning "to move." That is, emotions motivate action. Psychologist and philosopher William James said: "The emotions aren't always immediately subject to reason, but they are always immediately subject to action." Simply, the more your future picture is exciting, moving and tangible, the more it motivates you to take action in that direction. For example, when I was a child I tried, in vain, to learn to ride a bicycle. I would get on the bike, pedal a little and fall. No fun at all. For a while I let it go and I gave up trying to ride, until one day I imagined myself getting on the bike and riding safely. The picture was so palpable and bright, and it felt so real to me that I knew I had just learned to ride a bicycle. I left the room at once, went out, got on the bike and rode.

Amy Purdy, a young snowboarder who became severely ill at the age of nineteen, after which she lost both her kidneys and legs, describes how she came back to life after a long period of depression:

> I began to daydream. I daydreamed like I did as a little girl, and I imagined myself walking gracefully, helping other people through my journey, and snowboarding again. And I didn't just see myself carving down a mountain of powder, I could actually feel it. I could feel the wind against my face, and the beat of my racing heart, as if it were happening in that very moment. And that is when a new chapter in my life began.

Later on, Amy received artificial legs suitable for snowboarding, returned to professional sports and won a world championship gold medal!

Do not be alarmed if, at first, you find it difficult to visualize a successful future picture, or if your ambitions are modest, or you aren't enthusiastic about the future you imagine. Sometimes, our strength of will has been crushed and has atrophied over the years, so that we have learned to suppress any desire and hope for a promising future. It might take you a while to recover shelved enthusiasm and to let go of any cynicism and bitterness that resulted from past disappointments.

There are many ways to create a positive vision of the future, for example, through writing, drawing or imagination. The following exercise will instruct you how to create a vision through building a clippings collage. I especially love this exercise because it does not require any artistic talent and it's easy to get inspiration from tangible pictures and sentences. Many people find it easier than imagining a desired future. In general, I love using art because it allows us to bypass the literal walls to which we are accustomed and it connects us to our creative resources.

EXERCISE:
Building a vision through collage

Materials: a large piece of cardboard, colorful magazines and newspapers, a sheet of paper, scissors or a craft knife, glue.
Allow yourself at least 45 minutes of quiet time to construct the collage.

Follow these steps:

1. *Look in newspapers, magazines and periodicals for pictures that express your hoped-for self. Cut them out. You might also incorporate words or phrases that express your desired future and that inspire you. Do not try to be too sensible; listen to your intuition. If objections or critical voices arise, just write them down on a piece of paper, so you give them vent, and move them out of your way. Continue clipping images.*

2. *When you feel that you have enough pictures and sentences, select those images and words that best express the life you want to lead, the job you want to pursue, and your talents and added-value as an employee or a service provider.*

3. *When you are ready, paste the pictures on the cardboard. Listen to your feelings and your heart.*

> 4. *Display your collage where you will see it frequently.*
>
> *You may feel a need to update your vision after a certain period of time. If you feel that way – do it, but not more than once a month or three weeks at the most. You will see that the more you progress in achieving your goals, the more your future image will become accurate and ambitious. Over time you will achieve a clear and well-based future image, and will need to update it less frequently.*

The curse of success

One of the stressful factors that can sometimes eliminate joy from our lives is ... success. There is a traditional Jewish saying: "The more possessions, the more worry," which means wealthy people may be concerned about losing what they have already achieved, rather than enjoying what they have. Similarly, many successful people report that sometimes success is the biggest curse, especially if it came quickly and extraordinarily. For example, Joseph Cedar, an Israeli film director whose movies *Beaufort* and *Footnote* were nominated for the Oscar for Best Foreign Language Film, once said how he felt a lot of pressure after *Beaufort's* nomination to live up to the high standard he had achieved, and how this pressure to succeed can damage creativity.

The danger is greater especially in cases of very fast and large-scale success. It is no coincidence that a relatively high percentage of people in the entertainment business suffer from addiction, an above-average divorce rate and early death. Professor Mark Bellis from Liverpool John Moores University found that the output period of many artists is often very intense and short, and some do not live long afterwards. For example, Mozart died at the age of thirty-five, and Schubert at the age of thirty-one.

Our era has the notorious "27 Club" of popular musicians who died at the age of twenty-seven, often as a result of substance abuse. The 27 Club includes Jimi Hendrix, Janis Joplin, Jim Morrison, Kurt Cobain, Amy Winehouse and many more. In 2007, Bellis conducted a comprehensive study on the life expectancy of more than a thousand musicians who have achieved commercial success in the past fifty years. He found that the earlier in life those musicians attained success, the sooner their careers ended.

This phenomenon might be understood in different ways. Maybe fear of relinquishing achievements and acclaim raises anxiety to a dangerous level. It could be that achieving success is a habit and pattern of behavior, and it takes time to learn how to maintain it while also retaining a mental balance. And perhaps beliefs about oneself, like, "I do not deserve to succeed," or "Inside I'm just a loser," generate dissonance when success does occur, so the path to self-destruction is short. In any case, one thing that helps to deal with success is to regard it with the wisdom of perspective, not let it define who we are, and not accept it as a condition to our self-esteem. Once we were kids, without professions or money of our own, and one day we will die. Everything in between is adventure and, even, a game.

EXERCISE:
Giving yourself permission to be happy

What inhibits your joy? Do you really allow yourself to be happy? Do you feel it is safe to be happy?

Many people want to be happy, but at the same time they are afraid of it. They are afraid that if they are not sufficiently worried, things will not work out properly. Or, they might be afraid of being happy knowing the threat of losing what they had achieved.

The following exercise is designed to identify any inhibitions to happiness: Write this title at the top of a page:
15 bad things that will happen to me if I am happy.

Write down all the answers that come to mind, even if something seems silly or unreasonable. Do not judge any answers that pop up.
This exercise will give you a real opportunity to get to know the internal factors, difficulties and fears that hinder your joy, and unconsciously steer your life.

A key for success: taking life easy

One of the secrets to meaningful and creative careers is to manage that elusive balance between control and letting go, between exertion and relaxation. Surely, you view your career as having an important and meaningful purpose that can benefit you and others, and you really want to promote it. However, you want to be peaceful, happy and calm.

How do you do it?

In a meditation course led by teacher Joseph Goldstein, one of his students asked him: "What is your secret to attaining higher spiritual levels?"
The room went silent in anticipation of Goldstein's deep mystical insight, and he replied: "I do not take myself too seriously."

Being light and playful is the secret to creative life. Steve Jobs, the legendary founder and CEO of Apple Inc., also recommended this attitude and he strived to apply it to his own life: "Stay Hungry. Stay Foolish. I have always wished that for myself," is one of his famous quotes.

When I launched my own business I suffered from great emotional stress. I knew my savings would barely keep me going for seven months, and felt there was no way my business would pick up during that period of time. I turned to business coaches and went to marketing workshops. I built an annual plan and set weekly and daily goals. I looked for solutions and guides to help me, but all these, I felt, only amplified my feeling of helplessness. I did not know what else to do, so I signed up for a weekend meditation workshop on joy.

In one of the sessions we practiced meditation while walking on the grass outside. The teacher instructed: "Feel the damp grass beneath your feet, and let yourself be a 'nobody'. Do not be a 'somebody'. Forget all your stories and all your concerns. Let go of your identity." So we strode there, barefoot on the damp grass. A group of people of all ages and from all walks of life: young, old, senior executives, unemployed, women, men, healthy, sick. We all walked quietly, thoughtfully, on the green grass, trying to put aside our identities, and be a nobody for a whole hour. The rays of the sun caressed us and the birds chirping escorted our silent meditative walk. For me it was a moment of wild happiness. I felt like a child, carefree and light, and that all I had to do was walk on the grass and be there in the moment. I felt so vividly how the quality of "being in the here and now" is directly related to the ability to put aside stories and concerns, and let go of the past and the future. This is the key that allows the present moment to burst out with full force.

When I returned from the weekend I noticed a real miracle had occurred: my tension and stress had completely vanished! I still knew there was a chance I wouldn't succeed, but that didn't look like the end of the world to me anymore. My creativity was rekindled. The grave, fateful emotional burden that had hung over my head before the weekend was gone, and I could once again enjoy what I chose to do.

There is a famous saying: "Cemeteries are filled with indispensable people." That is, even the most important people in mankind's history or in our personal lives have died or will die, and the earth will continue to turn. In the same way, the world will still exist when we are gone. It may be hard to accept, but this a fact of life. The ability to let go of worries is partially related to trusting life, the universe, God, you name it, and a belief that reality is strong and smart enough to survive with or without us. If this is true, we can let life cradle us, just like a mother cradles her child, and be free to do what is really important – play, create, love, enjoy, do the best we can, and release control over what we can't do.

It is very important to take your life and your career seriously, and you certainly do that, but you should also learn to let go and relax control. Life is built upon this delicate balance between control and relaxation: we give and receive, work and rest, and our hearts contract and relax.

Meditation, bliss and finding purpose

Meditation helps us gain perspective. It reminds us to connect to what really matters, the foundation of our lives: breathing, bodily sensations, emotions, life itself as it is manifested at that very moment. Meditation helps us let go of worries, and see the fleeting and impermanent nature of things. Whatever comes, goes; and what goes, will come again. When you are occupied with building your career, dealing with financial and environmental pressures, and trying to balance professional life and family, it is important to occasionally observe a quiet moment.

Meditation practice is also a means of finding your balance again. It's about having a place set aside for connecting to your creativity, and it's a path leading to tranquility and inner peace. The American writer and mythologist Joseph Campbell gave a series of interviews on the PBC Broadcasting television network. In one of the episodes, entitled "Sacrifice and Bliss," he related to the importance of setting aside a few moments of solitude and silence, casting off obligations and just connecting to your inner self:

> *This is an absolute necessity for anybody today. You must have a room, or a certain hour or so a day, where you don't know what was in the newspapers that morning, you don't know who your friends are, you don't know what you owe anybody, you don't know what anybody owes to you. This is a place where you can simply experience and bring forth what you are and what you might be. This is the place of creative incubation. At first you may find that nothing is happening there. But if you have a sacred place, and use it, and take advantage of it, something will happen.*

Later in the interview, Campbell elaborated on how creating blissful moments will make life feel fresh. It will connect you to your purpose and help you find your path:

Our life has become so economic and practical in its orientation that, as you get older, the claims of the moment upon you are so great, you hardly know where the hell you are, or what it is you intended. You are always doing something that is required of you. Where is your bliss station? You have to try to find it. Get a phonograph and put on the music that you really love, even if it's corny music that nobody else respects. Or get the book you like to read...

If you follow your bliss you put yourself on a kind of track that has been there all the while, waiting for you, and the life that you ought to be living is the one you are living. I say, follow your bliss and don't be afraid, and doors will open where you didn't know they were going to be ... Wherever you are – if you are following your bliss, you are enjoying that refreshment, that life within you, all the time.

EXERCISE:
Observation meditation

One of the most effective methods to let go of worries and excessive self-importance is simple observation meditation. **Meditation is a way to recalibrate ourselves, to reboot, to let go of what is unimportant and simply connect to life.**
Studies show that meditation is also a very efficient tool for dealing with stress, especially when it is practiced on a daily basis over a longer period of time.

Sit in a quiet place where you are free from interruptions. Turn off the phone. Set an alarm clock for the time you have defined. It can even be just 5 minutes. Fifteen to 20 minutes is a recommended timeframe.

Close your eyes and assume a comfortable and well-balanced posture. You can either sit cross-legged on a mattress or on a chair. In any case, find a position that allows you to sit with your back straight but not stiff.

Pay attention to the natural movement of the breathing, to the incoming and outgoing air. Focus on the area where the breathing sensation is most dominant – it could be your abdomen, your chest or the nostril area.

Observe the physical sensations of breathing: the rising and falling and the expanding and contracting of the abdomen, chest, lower back or nostrils (depending on your focused area). You may also pay attention to the sensation of the air – whether it's warm or cold.

Do not try to control the breath; don't criticize it. Observe it objectively. Assume the position of the observer, the onlooker.

*A useful piece of advice is to treat meditation like a game. The meditation teacher Martin Aylward recommends adopting **the three C's approach: Care, Connection and Curiosity**. That's what matters. The goal of observation meditation is not to develop concentration but rather to learn to see and to accept what is. Developing awareness of breathing is only a means to learn to let go of all the other things (concerns, plans, and memories) and allow yourself to be exactly as you are right now. In this game there is no success or failure, but only what is happening at this very moment.*

If strong physical sensations arise, such as pain or discomfort, just let them be without any denial or struggle on your part, and return to observing the breathing. Usually these sensations will pass of their own accord after a while. If you feel these sensations take over the focus of your attention, and you feel you cannot return to focusing on the breath, shift attention to the distracting physical sensation and observe it for the next few minutes. This is not intellectual contemplation (interpretation, analysis or immersion in concerns), but rather taking the position of an onlooker, a witness, to the physical experience of the body.

If you feel you need to change positions, don't move fast or abruptly. Change position in slow motion, paying attention to the separate movements that comprise the transition between the postures.

Dealing with thoughts and emotions: our mind naturally tends to wander to thoughts, worries and plans. Various emotions, pleasant or unpleasant, can arise as well. In any case – as with physical sensations that arise during meditation – refrain from actively engaging with your thoughts and emotions. Let them be, with no intervention on your part, and return attention to breathing.

Again, if you feel emotions or if thoughts take over, you can adopt the position of the observer: say, for example, you feel anger, you can label it as "anger." Pay attention to the physical sensations that accompany the emotion.

The general guideline is to direct attention to the breath again and again without a struggle or a fight, but instead with acceptance and relaxation. At first, you may not be able to remain attentive to breathing for more than a few seconds. This is completely natural and there is no need to feel frustrated or worried about it. Remember that concentration and avoidance of thinking are not, as stated, the goal of meditation. Instead, the goal is letting go and accepting what is, all that there is. It's about being present without trying to change anything.

EXERCISE:
Meditation during the work day

The essence of observation meditation is to be present in this moment, accepting what is, and letting go of everything else. You do not have to make time for breathing meditation – although it might be useful to do so. Instead, or in addition, turn your breaks into meditation sessions. Do not be tempted to think that working continuously will improve your output. The opposite is true. So don't skip breaks during your day.

During a break, if you are alone, turn off the phone and just be present. Listen to the sounds of the street, look around, pay attention to your body and your posture. If you eat, do it attentively and slowly.
If you go out for a break with a colleague be 100% present in the conversation. Show interest, ask questions and truly listen. Do not talk about pressing matters at work. That is not the purpose of your taking a break.

A break does not have to be long but it should be of high quality. If you let go of worries and plans and be present in the moment, you will return refreshed and more productive to your work.

Remembering what matters; death as a wake-up call

Odelia Weinberg Perry, a meditation teacher, relayed to me a story that her teacher told her:

> *A man lived in New York in the 1970s working as deputy director of a bank, in charge of small business loans. He got tired of his life and sick of his work, so he decided to leave everything and go to an ashram in the East to find peace and serenity through meditation practice. After years of practice he returned to New York. One day, as he walked down the street, he ran into his former boss from the bank. The boss was delighted to see him back and offered him his former position as deputy director of the bank, in charge of small business loans. Our man thought and deliberated, and decided to take the job. He returned to the same place and the same job, but something significant had changed: he began to enjoy his work. Factors that once extorted him mentally – such as status, power games, manipulations, worries and pressures – no longer affected him. Only the essence, helping small business owners, remained – and that he loved to do.*

One of the things that help us remember the essence of things, what really matters in life, is awareness of our mortality. Steve Jobs, in his famous Stanford speech, spoke exactly of this: about the great liberation that lies in recognizing our finality, our inevitable death. He said that in the face of death only what's important remains. Pride, fear of embarrassment, the expectations of the world around us, everything fades in the face of knowing that life is short and the end is inevitable. We realize that we lose everything anyway, so there's no reason not to do what we love. Allow me to repeat what Steve Jobs said:

Remembering that I'll be dead soon is the most important tool I've ever encountered to help me make the big choices in life. Because almost everything – all external expectations, all pride, all fear of embarrassment or failure – these things just fall away in the face of death, leaving only what is truly important. Remembering that you are going to die is the best way I know to avoid the trap of thinking you have something to lose. You are already naked. There is no reason not to follow your heart.

Are you afraid of dying? Does the idea of your mortality depress or awaken you? I once read in a book by psychiatrist Irvin Yalom about his observations in his work with older people: those who were afraid and intimidated by death were usually the ones who felt they hadn't lived their lives to the fullest. If you are afraid of death – begin to live. Do not wait until old age.

The realization that my own death was unavoidable dawned on me when I was in my thirties. The hair that began to whiten and the facial lines I could no longer ignore depressed me on the one hand, but also woke me up. I decided to deliberately let go of old grudges, hang-ups and fears. I understand that life is too short not to live it to the fullest.

EXERCISE:
My life in retrospect

Instead of waiting for old age, you can right now imagine yourself looking back on your life when you're old and wise. It can help you connect to what really matters to you.

Find a few quiet minutes for yourself. Sit in a comfortable posture. Take some regular breaths and relax. Now imagine you're one hundred years old. Look back on your life and see that you have lived a life full of satisfaction and meaning.
What did you do that made your life full and rich?
What measures did you take in your career? In your personal life?
Give yourself a piece of advice as to how to improve your life now, so that it will be full of joy and inspiration.

Focusing on what you want rather than on how to achieve it

Joy, as mentioned, lies at the confluence between control and relaxation; between, on the one side, investing your heart and resolve to create a life and career full of substance, and, on the other side, letting go of what matters less and allowing yourself to release control. Control and release at the same time – it is a challenging and fascinating combination. In meditation practice it's done regularly, even on the posture level: sitting in an upright position and simultaneously relaxing the jaw muscles, shoulders and all tense body parts.

What does this combination mean to you? To your career?

Creativity expert Dr. Lucia Capacchione writes in her book *Visioning* about one of the secrets behind balancing control and release, which is focusing on "what" rather than on "how." The "what" of your life is your goal, your vision, which are the lighthouse that guides your way. However, it is important to let go of the "how." That is, remember that the road to achieving your goal is, like life itself, surprising, winding, full of twists and turns, and, especially, pretty much out of your control.

The more you invest your energy in "what," have a clear picture of what you want, and are committed to accomplishing your goal, and are still open to life's mysterious ways, the greater are your chances to achieve what you desire.

When my brother and I were neighbors, he brought home a new puppy. I was quite critical about how he raised him. He built a large cage in which the dog was isolated most of the day. The puppy didn't get accustomed to the new arrangement, and he cried for hours. His crying caused me great pain and my brother's attitude irritated me. My "what" was to help the dog get out of solitary, but I did not know how to do it. My attempts to discuss it with my brother were to no avail. He experienced them (and rightly so) as criticism, and he refused to listen to me. At some point I realized I had to let go of my intense attempts at persuasion, and try to open up to new ideas. Instead of talking my brother into acting differently, I decided to trust his love for the dog, even if I perceived it as "tough love."

When I let go of the criticism and reproach I came up with the creative idea of adopting a dog myself, and the two animals would be able to enjoy each other's company and play together. It was then that the most surprising thing happened: just one day after I started to play in my mind with the idea of adopting a dog (without sharing the idea), my brother informed me that he had decided to adopt another dog as company for his puppy. As soon as the two dogs got together they started playing happily, and the crying ceased.

Reality, it turns out, is much more creative than we believe it to be.

In this context, Buddha was once asked how he crosses the river. He replied: "Without stopping and without struggling." Whether you are starting a business or crossing the river, the principle remains the same: Keep your eyes on the ball and strive with determination to achieve your goal. However, along the way be open to whatever happens, don't struggle, and be creative. That's how you will reach your destination.

Focus on the process rather than the outcome

Another secret to balancing control and release, and a central key to successful and happy career life is focusing on the process rather than the results. When I lived in New York I worked for a couple who owned many real estate assets in Manhattan. They had come from low-income families, had built their lives with hard work, and became very successful in their own right. I once asked the woman what she enjoyed at work. Was it making money? Was it the ownership of the assets? "Neither," she answered, "Money for me is not the goal but a means to an end. I enjoy the action, and the adrenaline rush when doing business."

Many successful people share the understanding that joy is not found in the

destination but in the journey. Professor Randy Pausch concluded his "Really Achieving Your Childhood Dreams" lecture as follows:

> *So today's talk was about my childhood dreams, enabling the dreams of others, and some lessons learned. But did you figure out the head fake?*
>
> *It's not about how to achieve your dreams, it's about how to lead your life. If you lead your life the right way, the karma will take care of itself. The dreams will come to you.*

That is, if you live your life according to your values and you are determined to follow your heart, then your dreams will come true by themselves.

Career burnout

Sometimes it doesn't take a dramatic success or a major crisis to eliminate joy. Often it is routine that wears us down. What seemed enthralling and glamorous at first fades away and becomes gray. We get up in the morning to a work day that doesn't excite us any more.

Jonathan, a senior director in a commercial company, recounts:

> *At first it was difficult, stressful and even scary. In the evening I came home completely exhausted, but I felt great. After four years on the job the good feeling was gone. I lost my patience with everyone – my employees, my customers and also my wife and kids. But the most awful thing was that there was no apparent reason. I had become that kind of person who's bitter and angry all the time.*

Do you recognize this? When you embark on a new career, the first days, months, or years are full of glamour, challenge and joy. Like infatuation. However, sometimes, after a "honeymoon" period, routine takes over, and it paints the days with gray colors. You chose this particular career for all the right reasons; out of passion, a need for challenge, a desire to give to others and have an impact, but something has gone wrong along the road, and the dream of satisfying career life has never seemed more distant.

Jack Kornfield wrote a book about that, entitled *After the Ecstasy, the Laundry.* What was exciting at first becomes habitual, encompassing many small details and "dirty work." The challenge is gone, the initial excitement dissolved and a sense of meaninglessness and bitterness arises. It may be hard to admit, but all the efforts you invested to get to where you are seem ... redundant.

It's called burnout.

At present, this may seem to you like science fiction. You believe this will never happen to you, and you may even think, "I wish this were my problem." However, burnout is a very common phenomenon, especially amongst the most ambitious and highly motivated. It's worthwhile to pay attention at the outset, so as not to get to that point.

Professor Ayala Malach-Pines, a world-renowned expert on burnout research and co-author of *Career Burnout: Causes and Cures*, said in a 2011 interview for the newspaper *Calcalist*:

> *Thirty-five years of research have proven beyond any doubt that those who tend to burn out most frequently are those with the highest motivation in the beginning. These are the most enthusiastic, entrepreneurial, talented and caring people. The English language uses the term "burnout," and for burnout to occur, first there must be fire ... Burnout is when dreams of perfect execution are shattered. Cynics and unambitious people do not burn out.*

Factors of burnout

Some of the reasons for burnout are, as stated, **premature and very fast success** that is too much to handle, and therefore blocks creativity, or generates a feeling that after conquering the summit, "Where can I go from here?" But this is not the sole reason. Malach-Pines held interviews with more than ten thousand professionals worldwide, such as doctors, nurses, dentists, university professors, lawyers, insurance agents, directors and hi-tech entrepreneurs. She claims the most worn-out workers she met were the ones who performed the most caring and humanly significant jobs:

> *We detected the same phenomenon in any profession that employees saw as some kind of calling – policemen, doctors, psychologists, social workers ... that many of them become cynical over the years and now see their clients – those who at one time it was their lives' aspiration to help – as a kind of a hassle continuously trying to challenge their patience. I interviewed doctors who began to name their patients after their medical problems. I interviewed civil servants – municipal employees for instance – who said that they sometimes lock themselves up in their rooms for weeks, without saying hello to anyone, for fear that someone will ask them for something. I heard kindergarten teachers say: 'I'm tired of working with these little monsters.' These people chose these professions not because of the money – there is no money in them. They did it because they like people.*

According to Malach-Pines, one of the main reasons for burnout is a **buildup of emotions and feelings** like frustration, pain, shame, disappointment and failure, along with a sense of loneliness and not sharing their feelings.

Another factor of burnout is **loss of meaning in one's work.** It stems from neither long working hours nor physical and mental challenges, but rather from a feeling that one cannot fulfill their responsibilities, cannot realize their skills, and that one is wasted and worthless. Rona, a computer programmer in a large bank, said that what killed her inside and finally made her quit her job wasn't the programming ("which I loved"), but rather the outdated and ineffective work procedures in the work environment and lack of care on the part of the managerial team:

> *I was taken aback by what I experienced as totally ineffective lines of code. When I approached my manager and suggested a better way to write the code, he told me I was right, but nothing changed. After some more attempts I gave up. I realized that no one around me really wanted to work. Everyone, including the managers, came to work to do the very minimum, just to get their paycheck at the end of the month. I began to lose all motivation to go to work, I felt useless and worthless.*

Another significant factor of burnout is **loneliness and lack of social support.** We live in a world where human communication is more available than ever before. Social networks, internet services and mobile phones connect people with the click of a button. During the past few decades, technology has given us a world from which we can't disconnect, even for a split second. However, in this world of instant communication we suffer from unprecedented loneliness.

In the U.S. this phenomenon is more prevalent especially due to Relocation Stress Syndrome (RSS), because often changing a role or a job involves moving to another state. RSS is an officially recognized medical diagnosis which can include symptoms such as irritability, headaches and high blood pressure, and, in more severe cases, nightmares, panic, and the inability to focus on easy tasks at work. One of the risk factors for RSS is lack of social support. Relocated employees are far from their communities and original support systems, and they are susceptible to developing a sense of detachment and temporariness.

How to cultivate happiness at work and avoid burnout

As in any meaningful relationship, your relationship with your job requires constant nurturing. After the initial enthusiasm and the honeymoon period in a new job or career, routine begins, and there is a danger of boredom and accumulation of frustration and anger. If you want to enjoy your work in the long term, you should consider it as any other relationship, which requires constant care and attention.

Here are some ways to foster a rewarding relationship with your work. If you follow these principles while building your career, you will wear down less over time:

Remind yourself of the reasons you chose your work in the first place: Sometimes all it takes is to remember why you chose your career. Reconnect to your passion, your vision and the values that motivated you in the first place. Focus on what's important to you at work. Thus you will again find meaning in your job.

Make time at work for what really matters to you: Do not forget, even when you are busy with probably unavoidable "dirty work" (such as administrative matters), to make time for what makes you happy and satisfied. People tend to think of time in units of at least one hour. So, for example, if reading a book inspires us, we put off the idea because we do not have an hour of time to devote to reading. But even ten minutes of doing what you love can lighten your day. For me, writing is one of the most satisfying and creative aspects of my work. Even on busy days full of meetings and errands I dedicate at least 15 minutes to writing. Sometimes it's what makes all the difference for me between a significant day and just another day of work.

Deepen your relationships within and outside of work: A way to make your work meaningful is by creating better personal relationship with employees, colleagues and clients. If your job is mundane and unchallenging, this can make the difference. The psychologist Amy Wrzesniewski discovered that hospital cleaning staff who felt that their work was rewarding and fulfilling were the ones who talked and created relationships with patients and doctors at the hospital. Fostering close relationships with spouses, friends and family is one of the most important ingredients that will enrich your life and provide you with a network of emotional support, enjoyment and meaning.

Make it a regular practice to express your emotions: Journal writing offers therapeutic benefits. Keep an "emotions journal" and write in it whenever you feel burdened, stressed or gloomy. Release pent-up feelings to the fullest without criticism or judgment. Everything you feel – frustration, anger, guilt, helplessness, hatred, fear and pain – are all natural and normal. The best way to manage feelings is to release them on a regular basis.

Talk to friends or colleagues who understand and accept you. Also, a group of colleagues that meets regularly can be a great source of emotional support. Knowing that you are not alone, and that others go through similar things, will give you an emotional outlet and a sense of normalcy.

Professional enrichment and learning are extremely important, not only at the outset, but also when you are well established and even an expert in your field.

Balance between action and relaxation: meditate, take breaks, and go on vacations. Do fun things that nurture you emotionally, spiritually and physically: go to the beach, listen to music, spend time with friends, build a snowman.

The psychologist and creativity researcher Mihaly Csikszentmihalyi writes in his book *Creativity* that a part of the creative process is the incubation phase, when the creator lets go of the creative process. Ideas bubble beneath the threshold of consciousness, and form unexpected links. He cites examples of some of the most creative ideas that earned their creators with a Nobel

Prize and mentions that they came upon a vacation after a period of intensive work. Similarly, I find that my most creative ideas arise during meditation workshops, when I let go of work for a quiet weekend.

In addition to the joy that a balanced life brings, those moments when you let go of effort can result in a "quantum leap" in your career. Just when you loosen up, you might come up with completely new ideas that will advance you at once, and have much more impact than more hours of hard work.

Anger

Anger blocks creativity

Two weeks before the deadline to submit my M.A. thesis I was less than ecstatic, to say the least: my literature review amounted to only fifteen pages of the required twenty-five. My thesis composition had changed direction along the way, so I had already written dozens of pages that were no longer relevant to the subject. I found myself at an impasse, struggling for several days without any significant progress.

At that time my relationship with my mother was not particularly brilliant. My need for support during the thesis-writing just intensified my perception of her constant complaints and demands. I was in a bad mood, inclined to fight, and my mother certainly seemed like a worthy target. One day I exploded at her over the phone. I told my dad that I had no more patience for her egotism and that I just wanted her to leave me alone.

On about the third day of my writer's block, I realized that nothing good was going to emerge from me that evening, so I decided to go to a guided imagination and meditation workshop being held close to my home. In one of the exercises, the instructor asked us to imagine a safe place for ourselves in which we could relax during the meditation. To my surprise I found myself going to Jerusalem, to the home of my grandparents (who had died about twenty years earlier), to a small room at the back of their house. I remembered the house and the room, but I was not sure what was in this particular room and what it was used for.

Suddenly I realized it was my mother's childhood room. In my imagination I saw my mother as the little girl she was then, sitting on the bed, alone, and immediately I was filled with sadness and compassion for her. I always knew she had suffered through a difficult and lonely childhood; but that short moment when her sad, childish character appeared in my imagination provoked in me an understanding and compassion that I hadn't felt for a long time. The intense anger towards her that had accumulated inside me over the past few days just vanished. Strangely, this was the safe place that my mind chose during meditation.

On the way home, pieces of missing information started to fall into place. It was like mislaid pieces of a puzzle had been found and were creating new connections between the edited thesis content and the seemingly irrelevant material that I had cast aside. When I got home, around 11:00 p.m., I did some copy-and-pasting and added a few sentences, and before I went to sleep my thesis literature review constituted twenty-three pages!

One of the deepest insights I gained from that experience was that the feeling of being stuck is often associated with anger, guilt or criticism – towards ourselves or others, it doesn't really matter. Anger provokes internal inflexibility and fixation on issues such as: Who is right? Who is to blame? How do things need to be? Often we are not even aware of the hidden self-punishment mechanisms that come into play when we are angry.

For example, let's say you arrive back at the parking lot and discover that someone has hit your car and didn't leave a note. You feel angry and upset. You would probably agree with me when I say that this incident increases the chances that you will get angry at your spouse, spill coffee on your shirt, or get mad at the slow waitress in the restaurant. You may feel that the anonymous, terribly rude person who hit your car has "ruined your day," but what they really have done is beat up your car. Your day has actually been ruined by you, thanks to all the negative energy that anger brings with it.

This is not a judgmental statement. It's just how things are.

EXERCISE:
Clearing out feelings of anger

If you feel stuck, unproductive or angry, sometimes all you need to do is "release the valve" of the anger and move on. Stuck anger can really ruin your day.

If someone annoys you – be it a client, friend, family member or an HR representative – take a few quiet moments and write down what you feel. Even ten minutes can make a tremendous difference.

Through writing you might discover that other emotions, such as pain, arise. If so, you probably have revealed a deeper source of your anger stemming from previous injury. Continue to express whatever comes up.

After writing things down you might be able to put the incident behind you and continue your day, and you may even decide to contact or confront the person who has upset you. If necessary, continue writing over the next few days until you feel the anger has dissipated.

Anger in relationships and career

Sometimes the roots of feelings of angers it much deeper than a parking lot incident, and the results of the unprocessed anger can be much worse than coffee spilled on your shirt. Unresolved resentment and anger in significant relationships can sabotage your progress without your being aware of it.

Orenia Yaffe-Yanai, in her book *Career Your Passion,* describes cases where the lines between career and family are blurred, and dissatisfaction and frustration in one facet of life affects the other. For example, Yaffe-Yanai relates the story of Danny, a man who had left a successful job as a CEO to start his own business, but felt he had made a terrible mistake.

> *To be independent ... his words stuck in my ear. What exactly was his wish connected to? I asked myself over and over again.*
>
> *'So, maybe you wanted to be independent in another area of your life?'*
>
> *Danny curled into himself, and looked at me, shocked, as if he had been hit on the head with an ax: 'How is this relevant ...?' he muttered, without really asking.*
>
> *'Sometimes it is connected and confusing,' I said.*

Danny realized that his difficulties in his marriage had led him to "divorce" the wrong family – the "family" of the organization where he worked. When he recognized this, he returned to a job as an employee with a company, and tried to mend his marriage.

There is a complex dynamic between family relationships and career. In some cases, people (especially women) who have dedicated many years of their lives to taking care of their homes and children disrupt the family order because of a stalled career, for the family has become a symbol for lack of self-realization. In fact, after the problems at work are resolved, the family or marital crisis may disappear by itself.

Sometimes the roots of anger are much older and deeper, and are related to past relationships with parents that cast a heavy shadow on career choices in the present. In my work I met Michael, a talented and super-intelligent man who had failed to "find himself" and build a meaningful career. As a child Michael was a top student. He succeeded easily in school, and his proud parents hung his certificates of excellence on the refrigerator with unabashed pride. Michael received a B.A. with honors in economics, but since completing his degree he had wandered from job to job, from apartment to apartment, never staying in the same place for more than a year or two. Although Michael was highly respected in any position he filled, he always left for a trip abroad, or entered a period of unemployment, or started a job in a new field in which he had to start over from the bottom and work his way up. Both Michael and I were convinced that had he persevered long enough in the same job or even in the same field, he would have reached a high level of success.

Gradually it became clear that one of the significant factors of Michael's being stuck was a latent desire to avenge his parents, whom he experienced as insensitive, cold and detached. He felt they had cloaked him in the mantle of the excelling kid in order to glorify themselves, disregarding his real needs and desires as a child. Michael's experience was that of a rejected child, one who felt loved only because of his high achievements. "If I failed a test, and it did not happen often," he said, "my parents did not bother to hide their anger and their disappointment. They expected me to get back on track quickly and make them proud again." Michael felt used and unloved, and deep down inside he had developed an aversion to achievements, and gloated over the pain felt by his parents, who wondered where their talented kid had gone.

Closer scrutiny revealed that several factors had merged and negatively affected Michael's career. As a child he felt it wasn't legitimate to explore what he really wanted. Learning and academic achievements were considered of the highest importance, and everything else should be pushed aside. Thus he never asked himself what he really wanted to do. At the same time, Michael's deprivation of parental love, his deep-rooted pain and the intense anger bubbling inside were unconscious factors pressing him to become mired and fail professionally in order to hurt his parents – even at the cost of injuring himself. Another cause for his failure was his unconscious desire for his parents to finally accept him and, unconditionally, love him even as a "loser."

When Michael identified the anger, the hurt and the desire to get back at his parents, he understood that he had to release his anger and resentment from the past, accept the limitations of his parents and find out what he really wanted to do with his life.

Forgive and start over

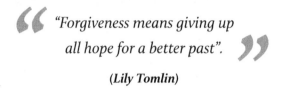

"Forgiveness means giving up all hope for a better past".

(Lily Tomlin)

If you really want to move forward to a better future, you need to let go of the past. It's time to release old injuries, to forgive parents who disappointed you or abused you or abandoned you. It's time to forgive friends who hurt you or strangers who trampled on you. It is also necessary to forgive yourself for injuries you have inflicted on others. Forgiveness is necessary, no matter how mild or severe the injury was. In point of fact, the severity of the injury does matter in one respect: the more serious it is, the greater the damage done, and hence the need for forgiveness is even more essential.

Forgiveness does not imply consent or approval of injustice and wrong actions. I'm talking about forgiveness that stems from recognizing the damage inflicted on you or by you and feelings of remorse. This increases the chance for repair: you might apologize, demand better treatment or leave things as they are.

Sound difficult? It is.

Forgiveness is one of the most courageous and demanding human actions. As Meher Baba, the Indian spiritual master, said: "True love is no game for the faint-hearted and the weak; it is born of strength and understanding," but it will set you free from anger and resentment and give you peace of mind. The negative energy of anger blocks the creative, lush and joyous flow of fertile activity.

It is important to remember another significant point in relation to anger and forgiveness: anger, fundamentally, is a protest against things that do not happen the way they should. The point is that life never goes exactly as we want, since life – like us human beings – is not perfect (although some philosophers would argue that it indeed is, but that's a discussion in itself). If we can't release and forgive others for their flaws, errors and negative actions, we will never be able to release ourselves from the grief and pain for all that is missing and flawed about us.

In the process of building a career it's common to experience anger towards people who let you down, reject you, or don't support you when you feel they should. It is also common to be angry at yourself about bad choices, missed opportunities and lack of motivation. However, resentment won't get you anywhere. If someone has hurt you – work it out. You can either do it directly with them or with yourself (through a writing exercise or with a friend or therapist.)

Another good piece of advice is to reverse the anger altogether – send love from the depths of your heart to the person who has angered you: "I send you love and light, I wish you happiness and success and that you open up your heart to yourself and others, including me. I wish we open up to each other."

Most important is to forgive yourself. You are doing the best that you can, as you always have. Self-flagellation and criticism are deeply ingrained habits for many of us (I'm quite familiar myself with the urge to slap my own wrists – if not worse), but usually compassion and encouragement are much more constructive.

FORGIVENESS EXERCISE

The following exercise is based on the practice of forgiveness in the Buddhist tradition, and it is divided into three parts: asking forgiveness of those you've hurt, offering forgiveness to those who've hurt you and seeking forgiveness of yourself.

Use this exercise to deal with your pain and hurt during your career-building, or in other aspects of your personal and professional life.

Find a quiet place. Sit comfortably, close your eyes and breathe naturally. Allow yourself to relax.

Asking forgiveness of others:
Repeat the following words: "If I offended or harmed anyone consciously or unconsciously, intentionally or unintentionally, I ask for their forgiveness." Allow yourself to recall those events when you hurt others, to see the pain you inflicted due to your own confusion and suffering. Feel the sorrow and regret that arose in you and, finally, ask for forgiveness: "I ask for your forgiveness."

Offering forgiveness to those who hurt you:
Repeat the following words: "If someone hurt or harmed me, consciously or unconsciously, intentionally or unintentionally, I forgive them." Recall the cases in which people hurt you or harmed you and the pain you have carried as a result. When you feel you are ready, repeat the words "I forgive you."

Seeking forgiveness of yourself:
Repeat the following words: "For all the ways in which I hurt or harmed myself, consciously or unconsciously, intentionally or unintentionally, I forgive myself." Recall the various ways in which you hurt or harmed yourself. Feel the sorrow you have caused yourself, feel your regret and remorse, and repeat the words "I forgive myself."

Don't be judgmental: During the exercise, emotions such as guilt, anger, doubt or a sense of betrayal may arise. Try not to judge yourself if this happens; these are natural feelings. Part of the process of forgiveness is to connect with the pain, anger and sorrow you carry. Note the different emotions that arise in you, and gently direct your attention back to practicing forgiveness. Have compassion for your resistance, and for the guilt, injured or angry feelings within you.

Forgiveness cannot be forced or artificial: If you feel that a certain incident or person is too challenging right now for the forgiveness practice, let it go.

Start with milder cases where you can forgive relatively easily. The process is gradual. In time, you will forgive yourself and others for more serious injuries. Forgive just yourself if you feel you are still not ready to let go and move on.

There is considerable power in our intentions: So if you sit in meditation in order to forgive, remember that the intention is the most important thing, even if at times you feel mostly anger or sorrow. Gently touch these emotions and remind yourself of your good heart and the pure basic intentions with which you came to practice. Find comfort in the good heart with which you sat down to meditate.

Guilt

Ethics and business

In the film *Matchstick Men* Nicolas Cage plays Roy, a professional con man from Los Angeles who finds different ways to "sting" people and trick them into giving him their money. Roy develops obsessive-compulsive disorder stemming from, as it turns out later, inevitable pangs of conscience related to his line of work.

The world of career and the world of ethics are two domains with a complex relationship. Wherever money is involved, a tendency towards greed, exploitation and fraud arises. Making a living touches upon the issues of existence and survival, and it is sometimes difficult to refuse an opportunity to make money, even when it comes with a certain moral price. Examples of ethics in business issues are tax fraud, worker exploitation, delivery of sub-quality products, falsified reporting of working hours and, of course, larger issues such as animal testing, weapons trade and environmental pollution.

In essence we have a moral yardstick that tells us when we do wrong and when we do right. **A lack of integrity and morality holds us back from leading lives embodying long-term success as well as happiness and peace.** Building a successful and satisfying career requires peace of mind, emotional freedom and the self-confidence that only honesty and integrity can impart. The price of guilt is internal noise.

Buddhist psychology talks about the concept of karmic cause and effect: every action we perform is a seed we sow now that will yield future fruit with the same seed we have sown. In other words, any action that causes suffering to you or to others would inevitably, in the present or future, cause more suffering.

Dr. Gerald Epstein, a psychiatrist and expert in mental and physical healing through guided imagery, describes some of the conditions necessary to go through a successful healing process. According to Epstein, one of the basic conditions for physical and mental health is cleansing, which means maintaining physical and ethical cleanliness. In order to be healthy we must ask ourselves how clean we are in our contacts with others and with ourselves. "The body does not lie" means that any moral or ethical deviation is registered in our body. This can adversely affect our physical and emotional lives. Epstein testifies from his clinical experience that there exist connections between mental/physical illness and immoral behavior, as well as the resulting emotions, such as guilt and self-punishment.

Guilt creates self-punishment mechanisms and produces internal noise, like ropes holding us down. This, in turn, can really disrupt us from breaking through and expressing ourselves fully. According to Buddhist teacher Ajahn Chah those who live a moral life have a quiet heart. Similarly, in Suttanipata, one of the Buddhist scriptures, the Buddha says: "There is one whose mind is clear – the one whose action in the world of senses is pure and good." That's the reason we use the phrase "sleep peacefully at night" when we discuss whether a deed is moral or not. Immoral actions disrupt restfulness and disfigure inner peace and happiness. Internal conflict sabotages quiet and clear action. A really successful and satisfying career promotes satisfaction, happiness and security, while dishonesty undermines the foundations of these feelings.

Another element related to morality is the interdependence of our lives in and with the world. The Buddhist perception, like many other spiritual teachings, emphasizes the interrelationship between all things; everything is affected by everything, so when we hurt another person we hurt ourselves too. Philosophy professor Dr. Frogel defines ethical action as "an action that promotes the happiness of the society and the individual." This interdependence is nicely illustrated in an ancient Jewish fable:

> *A group of people were sitting in a boat. One of them took a drill and began to drill a hole underneath himself. His companions asked him: 'What are you doing?' and he replied: 'What concern is it of yours? Am I not drilling under my own place?' They said to him: 'But you will flood the boat for us all!'*

That is, every action we take influences others in some way, it reverberates in the world, and the results will come back to us again in the end.

Advanced managerial perceptions of career as one aspect of holistic and happy living stress the importance of living morally if you wish to enjoy a long-lasting, prosperous and successful career. Management expert Ken Blanchard and Peale Norman, one of the founders of positive thinking, collaborated in their book *The Power of Ethical Management* to illustrate and explain the principle of ethics in business. The two emphasize that you do not have to lie in order to win, and that fairness pays off. They give practical advice for ethical decision-making with a view to generate profits and success over time.

Likewise, Rami Levi, one of the most prolific and accomplished businessmen in Israel, says that being honest has been one of the keys to his success. Levi was reared in a poor family with many children. He broke into the Israeli market with retail food shops with particularly low prices, low profit margins and large sales volume. By 2011, his chain of stores had become the third largest in the country and accounted for about 7% food market share. At a 2013 conference on Business Success when Levi was asked about the key to his success in business he replied: "Ethics comes for me before professionalism."

He elaborated: "Be honest, reliable, and without unnecessary manipulation, this will leverage the results."

Given today's global village and the abundant availability of information, when so many aspects of our lives, both private and professional, are exposed to all through social networks, blogs and search engines, it is twice as important to be transparent, reliable, and conscious of maintaining a good reputation. Holding fast to our values as professionals is key to attracting customers and clients – and most importantly – to sleeping well at night.

Amendment and forgiveness

If you have undertaken immoral deeds in the present or past, it is important to fix what you can so as to cleanse the guilt together with all its muddy sediments. Only then can you move on with a clear and quiet conscience. I love the Buddhist definition of unethical deeds, as it is broad enough to leave room for personal discretion, and yet it provides the basic guidelines for ethical conduct. Buddhist psychology sets five dictates: a moral person should avoid lying, stealing, killing, sexual misconduct and the use of intoxicants that blur awareness (although I personally think that a drink here and there is OK.).

I recommend that you cease any immoral actions that you are involved in, **even if they are not directly related to your career**. If you have hurt or wronged anyone, it is important to fix what you can, like returning money you took dishonestly or compensating for damage you caused. In addition, if it's possible, ask the forgiveness of those you've wronged. If you cannot turn directly to the offended person, go through the process of asking for their forgiveness indirectly by writing a letter or through guided imaginary meditation. Finally, forgive yourself. In the chapter on anger there is a detailed exercise that deals with the process of forgiveness.

Feelings of guilt and low self-esteem

Sensitive people or people with low self-esteem sometimes suffer from guilt about events and incidents that are outside of their accountability. For example, in the Grief & Loss chapter, I depicted a mother who felt guilty about the death of her son from illness. A typical symptom of people who were neglected or abused in childhood is a tendency to assume blame and take responsibility for their parents' behavior. Also, children who experienced the divorce of their parents may suffer from the effects of guilt from not being able to hold the family intact. In all these cases, and in many others, feelings of guilt have a destructive effect, even if their source is clearly unjustified.

People working in therapeutic professions may sometimes hold themselves excessively accountable and feel unjustified guilt. Doctors, psychologists, teachers, social workers and anyone working in the treatment of people may see themselves as responsible for the failure of a given treatment, even if the spectrum of reasons for failure is much broader than the actions of the therapist. Harboring feelings of guilt and excessive responsibility can severely damage the therapists' quality of life, adversely affect their personal relationships and sabotage their professionalism. This can cause them to suffer from emotional burnout and loss of energy at work.

Another common phenomenon of taking blame is the one experienced by working women towards their children regarding the balance of career and family. Of course men may suffer from similar feelings of guilt. There is no easy way to deal with these feelings. It is important to examine the prioritization of your values, checking that you do the best you can within your familial and economic constraints. Remember that your satisfaction and self-fulfillment are also important. Orenia Yaffe-Yanai says that a professionally frustrated parent causes mental harm to both himself and his children, who receive the message that self-realization is difficult or prohibited. The children then take this message into adulthood. I've worked with groups in which I saw a high correlation between the participants' self-realization and that of their parents.

People who found it difficult to give themselves internal permission to dream and to realize their dreams usually came from families where at least one parent was unfulfilled and professionally frustrated.

It is very important to maintain therapeutic and professional boundaries with clients. In cases of therapeutic failure it is worthwhile to seek a sympathetic ear with another therapist or with a support group of colleagues, or to use your social support network – whether it's friends, your spouse or other family members. Do not stay alone! In the case of guilt, as with other difficult emotions like anger, grief or fear, it's good to also allow yourself an emotional outlet through writing, for example, through the following exercise.

EXERCISE:
Cleansing feelings of guilt

Writing a letter to the person you feel you've wronged can help you to release your emotions. Emotional release will allow you to see new aspects of the situation that you might not have grasped before (feelings of guilt have the ability to blur all perspectives other than your self-blame). Emotional release will allow you to make an informed decision regarding your next steps.

There is no need to send the letter to the recipient. Writing is often enough in itself.

The guidelines for writing a letter like this are simple:

Allow ample room for your guilt feelings. *Do not hesitate to use words like "I'm sorry, I feel responsible for …," "I regret …," "It hurt me when …," and so on.*

If more feelings come up – such as anger, sadness, disappointment and fear – give them full expression. *For example, you might discover that you also harbor intense anger towards the person to whom you are writing the letter. It is natural; guilt and anger are emotions that often intertwine.*

It is very important to express feelings of love and forgiveness. *Even if the guilt overwhelms you, keep on writing until, inside yourself, you find understanding, forgiveness and love for yourself and/or the subject of the* *letter. Love and care are the foundation of your guilt. Had you not cared, you would not have felt any pangs of conscience. Do not finish the letter until you get to feelings of love. On the other hand, do not force yourself or express love artificially. Eventually, after you give vent to feelings of grief, regret and anger, love will sprout through the cracks. Continue writing the letter – even if the writing takes you several days – until you also reach love and forgiveness.*

Self-love and letting go of guilt will boost your energy

Guilt can be an engine for positive action, but it comes with a price tag. The film *Machine Gun Preacher* depicts the true story of Sam Childers, an American man who dedicated his life to saving children in the north of Sudan from the malign harm of the Lord's Resistance Army (LRA), an organization that was responsible for the murder and rape of children or their exploitation as child-soldiers. One scene in the film shows how Childers' pain, distress and helplessness caused him to lose control in anger at his wife and daughter, who wanted to continue to live normally and spend money on life's pleasures. At that moment he felt so guilty and powerless that he could not allow himself or his family a moment of peace to enjoy their good fortune.

One of the reasons that it is difficult to let go of guilt, shame or concern is our belief in the positive power of these emotions to drive us to act in ways that are beneficial to ourselves or others. Deep in our hearts we fear that if we stop feeling guilty, it means that we don't care anymore. We are afraid that the opposite of guilt is indifference, and the opposite of worry is complacency. You have probably heard the saying that "The way to love another is to first love myself," but somewhere deep down inside that might sound to you like a cliché, and maybe, sometimes, even an excuse for egotism.

One of my teachers in high school talked about **self-love as being like a cup you fill up with water until it overflows, and spills everywhere.** That, he said, is self-love. You are filled with so much love that ultimately it must affect everyone around you. If you are not full of goodness, wisdom, peace, love, what can you give to others? That is, if you want to give, it is no less important that at the same time you make sure to provide your own needs: security, stability, peace, calm, love. For example, some people experience a breakthrough in their career only after they have found love in their personal lives. This is what happened to Yonit Werber, a successful personal and business-success coach. Yonit is an engineer by training, and holds a M.Sc. in information systems management. After her husband died unexpectedly in a work accident when she was twenty-five, she switched to art therapy, but this did not feel like the most fitting professional choice either. She said:

> When I finished working as an art therapist because I felt that it was no longer right for me, I asked my therapist why it had to take me so many years and so much to study just to realize that again it wasn't the right profession for me. She told me it was because I had to first rebuild the things that were even more important to me, such as a new family.

Yonit had expressed her desire to first and foremost restore the family aspect. Her career breakthrough occurred after she got married again and her first daughter was born. In other words, we need to stock our energy supplies, in any way that works for us, to be able to engage in productive activity that's beneficial to ourselves and others.

When you're "good", it's good for others too

Another way to understand the importance of self-love is through what is known in psychology as "projection," or through the spiritual notion that the world around us is created by our perception of it. Our view of the world is not objective, but rather dynamic and full of interpretations and biases, and we are drawn to see things in reality that match our perception of the world. It is easy to demonstrate it in terms of relationships. For example, Ms. A. that thinks all men want just sex, will find herself repeatedly involved with men who only want sex. However, Ms. B. who thinks men want to build a family, will more easily find a man to build a family with.

This can be explained by our selective attraction to people and events that reinforce our worldview, but also how we actively create our reality. That is, it may be that the same men would only want sex from Ms. A. and yet would want a serious relationship with Ms. B. Our unconscious beliefs and needs form a network of interaction with the beliefs and needs of others, and we respond to each other without necessarily being aware of what triggers us. We are not only passively attracted to people fitting our worldview, but we also actively cause others to respond to us as we believe they should.

We create the world around us in a dynamic and active way – as a projection of our inner perception of ourselves and reality. In this way, if our inner world is saturated with pain and sorrow, this is what we also perceive externally in our family, friends and clients. In a sense, and maybe it will sound a little outrageous to you, if we wear "glasses" of pain when we look at the world, then we also create pain on some level. However, when we transform the suffering and difficulty that exist within us into love, we will automatically change the world around us.

A dramatic example of this is the story of Dr. Hew Len, a psychologist who healed a ward of mentally ill criminals without having to meet any of them face to face, by using the ancient Hawaiian healing practice of *Ho'oponopono*. According to the method, problems result from painful thoughts or memories from the past, and the way of healing is that the therapist takes responsibility for the patient's problems. That is, he recognizes inside himself the painful or wrong parts that gave rise to the problem, then asks the Great Spirit to help him heal those parts, and in doing so he also cures the patient. According to *Ho'oponopono* the world is entirely your own creation, meaning that you are responsible for healing yourself so as to then heal whatever appears to you to be a problem.

Think about your own life experience and how your emotional state affected others around you. For example, recall a time your spouse was in crisis. Did you identify with their plight, and dwell in their pain? Or maybe you radiated love, joy and optimism? In which case did you better help your spouse? If you cannot remember ways you affected others, think about how others affected you.

A loving and radiating presence can eliminate the existence of pain and sorrow around it. This quality is called "empathy" or "compassion." Steven Folder, one of my Buddhism teachers, says that compassion is the place where our love meets the suffering of the other. Meeting the sufferings of others through empathy and not through identification is a much more beneficial way to help others without hurting yourself. Even if the pain and suffering of others do not disappear in our presence, empathy allows you to hold fast in a strong, stable and happier place. So all the more will you have a stronger and more sustaining foundation to be a real support to others, and help them deal with their suffering. It is much more difficult to support others when you carry the same load of pain. On a personal level, when I see repeating patterns of distress around me, I devote time to finding where this distress exists in me, and dedicating time and energy to curing it. This helps me to assist others from a much more powerful state, and with a better perspective on the situation.

Nurturing yourself and taking care of your spiritual, emotional and physical needs is good advice for anyone who comes in contact with suffering in his personal and professional life – and who doesn't? Let go of the inner voice that accuses you of egotism, and seal out the voices of others that rebuke you if you invest in yourself, your career and your happiness. My decision to fill my life and career with joy, peace and confidence also stems from the knowledge that I will have more resources to help others.

When you are cured, your environment heals as well.

Failure & Disappointment

Failing is a natural part of life

Sophia Loren once said: "Mistakes are part of the dues one pays for a full life." I believe this to be true. Mistakes, failures, and crises are an inevitable part of life.

Do you experience rejections as you build your career? Have you received negative responses from customers or from potential employers? Did you ever launch a product you couldn't sell? If so, you are not alone! Rejections, setbacks and mistakes are an integral part of any business or career-building process. The important and interesting question is not how to avoid failures, but rather how to manage them and deal with them when they happen. Yuval Eilam, the director of an educational center preparing youth for recruitment to elite units in the Israel Defense Forces (IDF), says: "I can say with certainty that dealing with failures is one of the most crucial issues in the preparation process." After more than twenty-five years' work as an educator he has come to the conclusion that "the ability to cope with failure or disappointment is one of the most important factors for those who want to succeed in life."

Failure is a daily occurrence, and the learning process involves trial and error. This is illustrated clearly in sports: missing a shot or a goal is part of the game. For example, a basketball player who scores between 20 and 25 points per game usually gets no more than 40% of his shots into the basket. That is, he misses more than he converts. A tennis player winning seven games to five misses at least half the balls in the game. Thus, missing the goal or being down to the opponent at times is an integral part of finally achieving success.

The acquisition of any skill, even those of the most complex sort – whether it's managing people, time, tasks, or, in fact, any of the skills you've acquired to attain professional status in your field – is not very different from the learning process of a baby taking his or her first steps. Falling is part of the story. It allows you to make adjustments and improve your skills as you advance along the path to becoming a professional. Thus, making room for mistakes is imperative in any learning process. For example, during my graduate studies we had a course called "Learning Lab," in which the purpose was to offer experimental facilitation of a group and provide authentic feedback. The professor defined the objective of the course as "extending an invitation to boldly make mistakes and get lost." The student's grade was based on his or her level of curiosity and desire to learn along the way, rather than on concrete results. This inspired me and gave me space to really explore what group facilitation meant to me. It allowed me to learn much more than I might have, had I instead been evaluated based on my success at leading a group.

If you think about it, the process of developing oneself into a professional is also a skill; all the aspects of marketing, sales, financial management, time management and setting goals and targets are acquired skills. It takes time, determination and patience to master them.

Fear of failure limits success

Many people experience errors and failures as destructive, dangerous and fatal. Most people are afraid to fail and that causes them to restrain their creativity, reduce their aspirations and set supposedly "realistic" targets that do not really inspire them.

The song The Rose describes the diminution of life that stems from the fear of losing, falling and failing:

> *It's the heart, afraid of breaking*
> *That never learns to dance.*
> *It's the dream, afraid of waking*
> *That never takes the chance ...*
> *And the soul, afraid of dying*
> *That never learns to live*

I know first-hand the fear of failure and minimization that comes with it. As a child I was a perfectionist. A typical example: in fourth grade I started to learn to play the piano, and was so demanding of myself that upon every mistake I made, I went back to the beginning of the piece until I played it perfectly. My parents would come to check if everything was okay because they heard me repeat the same piece over and over again, without a break. Later in life, excellence became an obsession and a double-edged sword for me. A strong starter, I skipped two grades in school, completed my B.A. degree with high honors and achieved some more wonderful successes. But then I was so afraid to fail that I chose to play it "safe," and to learn or do only those things at which I could excel. I chose to engage in areas where the risks were minimal, but neither did they challenge my abilities. While my friends progressed in their work, I chose jobs that were undoubtedly beneath my abilities. The price, in both emotional and economic respects, was heavy: I felt mired professionally and financially, and envied my friends for all the really interesting jobs they had.

Only in my early thirties did I begin to take significant risks in my career. This was also the beginning of the most significant breakthrough period of my life on a professional as well as a personal level. Today, I sincerely believe that it is better to try and fail than not to try at all. It's better to try and fail than to avoid. Today I take pride in a glorious list of failures, and I'm sure that list will grow.

OBSERVATION EXERCISE: *How do you perceive failures?*

Ponder what failures, mistakes and rejections mean for you:

Attitude towards failure: *Are you tormenting yourself over mistakes or do you see them as a lever for growth? Are you learning lessons from the mistakes and failures? Do you feel that failures discourage you rather than make you wiser?*

Beliefs: *How did your parents react to your failures when you were a child? Were you punished when you made a mistake or did you receive encouragement and reassurance? Does your family encourage risk-taking? Do you see a connection between your attitude towards failure and what you experienced within the family setting?*

Daring: *Do you avoid trying new things because you fear you will fail? Do you reject taking action until you are 100% sure of your capabilities, or are you a "dive-into-the-cold-water" type of person?*

Daring to fail – the courage to live

This view, that failure is a natural, necessary and even a positive part of life is deeply rooted in spiritual teachings and philosophies. Rumi referred to failures as part of life's journey:

> *Come, come, whoever you are.*
> *Wanderer, worshiper,*

lover of leaving.
It doesn't matter.
Ours is not a caravan of despair.
Come, even if you have broker you vows
a thousand times.
Come, yet again, come, come.

Spiritual teachers, poets and philosophers have seen a connection between inner freedom and liberation from fear of failing or falling. When I was a teenager in a youth movement we would merrily sing the song of Rabbi Nachman of Breslov: "All the world is a very narrow bridge, but the main thing is to have no fear at all."

Similarly, Mother Teresa prayed:

Deliver me, O Jesus: From the fear of being humiliated. From
the fear of being despised. From the fear of being rebuked. From
the fear of being slandered. From the fear of being forgotten.
From the fear of being wronged. From the fear of being
ridiculed. From the fear of being suspected.

My understanding of Mother Teresa is that only those willing to experience failures, mistakes, ridicule and reproach can experience true liberation to act upon their inner truth.

Certain concepts go even further and nullify the concept of "failure." According to these concepts only what is happening – the "here and now" – has meaning. Whether present experience is good or bad, acceptance of reality "as is" means letting go of expectations, wishes and desires, and being completely present in the moment. The psychoanalyst Wilfred Bion said that a good therapist should treat his patients "without memory and without desire," meaning: allowing them full freedom to be themselves, in all authenticity as they truly are. Being fully present in life requires losing control and letting go of expectations. Freedom to fail is the freedom to experiment. If what is happening now in reality is exactly as it should be, then the word "failure" loses its negative charge.

In Vipassana meditation, for example, there is no concept of failure. Even if attention wanders repeatedly, and concentration on breathing is lost over and over in the face of myriad thoughts and distractions, these are natural components of the meditation. Nurturing wisdom in meditation is understanding the nature of things as they are, including the pleasant, unpleasant, beautiful and ugly aspects. At the heart of it all there are no failures; there is life. If we learn to attribute a positive meaning to every occasion, to learn and grow from every event, we can live a much happier life and maintain a sense of substance and value even in difficult times. When we perceive failure as an inherent part of the circle of life, comprising successes, failures, repairs and so on, we can accept the momentary lapses in perspective. There's no need to invest unnecessary energy in making excuses, justifying ourselves or looking for someone to blame. Whatever happened has happened, and life continues its course.

EXERCISE:
The freedom to fail

Think about the different ways in which your fear of failure imposes restrictions on your life.

Now, think what your life would be like if you were living in an environment that encouraged creativity and fully accepted mistakes and failures. Sit in a quiet place and close your eyes. Take a few deep breaths and imagine a good fairy who tells you:
"Allow yourself to create and to do whatever you want. It's OK to fail, and it's OK to be wrong. Everything is fine."

Write down all the plans that you come up with during the exercise.
Choose from the list at least one thing to be completed in the coming week or month.

If you find it difficult to let go of the fear of failure and do the exercise, I recommend trying the opposite approach:
Ask yourself: "What's the one thing I would do if I knew for sure I would succeed at it?"

> *The beauty in asking the opposite question is that it frees you from the fear of failing and overrides objections that perhaps arose with the first question, because it operates on the (imaginary) assumption that you are going to succeed anyway.*
>
> *Do this exercise once a week.*
>
> *If you are a perfectionist this exercise is especially important for you. It will help you see new possibilities, release pent-up energy, and allow you to come up with new ideas.*

Failure – a teacher for life

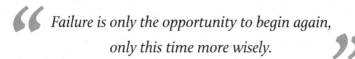 *Failure is only the opportunity to begin again, only this time more wisely.*

(Henry Ford)

One of the significant characteristics of successful people is not their lack of failures, but the ability to see them as a lever for growth and learning, as an opportunity to continue to vigorously expand their activities. Successful people know that mistakes and failures are part of the learning process. They take responsibility for failures, and learn from experience to further enhance their knowledge and skills and to work even better in the future.

In their book *Success Built to Last,* based on a six-year research project into what makes enduring great companies, Emery, Porras and Thompson state that successful organizations always provide an environment that enables learning and repair and "forgives" mistakes. The authors came to the unequivocal conclusion that successful companies are those that inscribe constant lesson-learning on their banner, and that consider failures a part of the process of continuous improvement. The following remarkable example illustrates how far-reaching and revolutionary this idea is. There is a story about Jack Welch, the legendary CEO of General Electric, who once had a manager who made a business mistake that cost the company ten million dollars. When the manager handed Welch his letter of resignation, Welch handed it back to him and said: "I just paid ten million dollars for your tuition. Why would I want you to go work for my competitors?"

Think about what your career would look like if you adopted this attitude towards your failures!

Giving yourself and others permission to make mistakes, take risks and fail opens so many new possibilities in your career development. It will unleash your creativity and allow you to be original and unique and to shine with your brightest colors. Truly outstanding companies are experts at failure. They apply a system of continuous learning and improvement in cases of failure. The rationale is this: to really succeed you have to dare. Innovation, in essence, requires trial and error and risk-taking, as Albert Einstein once said: "Anyone who has never made a mistake has never tried anything new." Organizations (or people) who refrain from taking risks might make fewer mistakes, but they won't create really innovative things. Hence, the way to succeed is not to avoid making mistakes but to make new mistakes every time!

In summary, trial and error are necessary ingredients for producing success. There is no such thing as long-term success without failures and lessons learned for future improvement. Anthony Robbins, the renowned business coach, said: "Success in life is the result of good judgment. Good judgment is usually the result of experience. Experience is usually the result of bad judgment."

EXERCISE:
Learning from failure

If you failed or made a mistake, ask yourself the following questions to determine the cause of failure and to draw conclusions for the future:

1.   Why did it happen? What was the real cause of failure?

2. *How can I prevent a recurrence of the incident?*

3. *If it happens again, how should I deal with it?*

It is also important to ask yourself two more questions:

4. *What are the positive aspects of this situation?*

5. *What can I learn from this experience?*

These last two questions are based on the assumption that every one of life's events can help you learn and grow. These questions shift the focus of attention to the potential benefits inherent in a given situation. Focusing on these questions will enhance your positive frame of mind and help you see that every situation holds the potential for learning and growth. Positive feelings can help you to be more creative and energetic. This, in turn, facilitates coping with failure.

Sometimes it is easier to understand the contribution of setbacks and crises through the lens of time:

Think of a professional crisis or failure that you experienced in the past:

1. *What did you learn from this experience?*

2. *In what ways have you grown as a result of the failure you experienced?*

3. *Write down at least five ways in which this experience contributed to your personal and professional growth.*

Remembering to learn lessons and take away new insights from failures is a good habit that will help you better deal with mistakes, failures and crises.

Determination and perseverance are key factors for success

> *There is no failure except in no longer trying.*
> *There is no defeat except from within,*
> *no really insurmountable barrier*
> *save our own inherent weakness of purpose.*
>
> **(Elbert Hubbard)**

Naftali Bennett, a politician and a high-tech entrepreneur, made the deal of a lifetime when his start-up company Cyota was acquired by RSA Security Inc. for the legendary sum of 145 million dollars when he was only thirty-three years old. However, success was not instantaneous; the company's very profitable product – an algorithm for preventing online fraud – was only developed following two years' investment in another product that totally failed. If the company owners and investors had given up after the first attempt, they would never have reaped the rewards of their investment.

It's not enough to be talented, not enough to have a good idea, and not enough to have a perfect business strategy. All of these are certainly important, but the main, if not the most essential, drivers of success are determination and perseverance. Calvin Coolidge, the thirtieth president of the United States, said:

> *Nothing in this world can take the place of persistence. Talent will not; nothing is more common than unsuccessful men with talent. Genius will not; unrewarded genius is almost a proverb. Education will not; the world is full of educated derelicts. Persistence and determination alone are omnipotent. The slogan "Press On" has solved and will always solve the problems of the human race.*

Determination and perseverance mean picking yourself up and starting anew, over and over again, regardless of setbacks, crises, self-doubt and the doubts of people around you. The reason why many people fail to achieve their objectives is that they lack determination and perseverance. They give up too soon in the face of an initial (or second or third) failure and stop trying. In my work I have come across many people who believed that if their idea was good, it would succeed – and fast. If it failed, they often thought that it was probably not a good idea to begin with, or maybe they felt they were not talented enough.

However, the biographies of successful people show that this is not always the case. Some of the greatest artists, scientists, businesspeople and politicians have struggled to achieve recognition in their early days, and some of the most spectacular successes were achieved with sweat, determination and self-trust in spite of many obstacles. Some examples include the Beatles who were rejected in 1962 by the Decca record company, whose executives said, "Guitar groups are on the way out" and "The Beatles have no future in show business." Other famous artists that were rejected, some of them over the course of many years, include author J.K. Rowling, actor Sylvester Stallone and singer Jon Bon Jovi. The animator and businessman Walt Disney wound up bankrupt from his first endeavor. Another example, this time from the field of politics, is Abraham Lincoln, who was elected president of the United States in 1860 after a series of family, career, and political crises.

In short, even if you have a great idea and you are also extremely talented, you may still have to prove yourself over and over again in order to succeed and gain recognition. Failures and rejections are not an indication that you should stop, but natural and inevitable bumps on life's path for anyone who gets up in the morning and tries to do something meaningful. I love the saying of Winston Churchill: "Success is the ability to go from one failure to another with no loss of enthusiasm," i.e., determination is your success. Even if you fall a thousand times, being devoted to your cause, having a positive attitude and believing in yourself and your vision are already a success, which is certain to yield real fruits in the future.

Dealing with failure requires a lot of courage. It's easy to despair, look for someone to blame and cry over your bad luck. However, successful people know that failure is also an opportunity: those who know how to overcome setbacks without losing confidence are usually the ones that succeed in their professional and personal lives. In other words, personal and business success is achieved when we understand that we must do, apply, invest and persevere. Do not look for shortcuts. Many of the world's most significant accomplishments were achieved by tired and discouraged people who kept on trying.

Being stuck as an expression of inner conflict

Okay. So we get it that determination is essential to succeed, right? But what do you do when you feel that you are fighting against windmills? What should you do if you feel deep down inside that it's more than just a setback? When you feel that something is stuck? That it's not merely difficulties along the way, but something really does not work?

If this is what you feel, and only you know if it is so, you should look inside yourself.

When the road is difficult and full of potholes, when something's repeatedly not working, when you feel something is just not right and reality is throwing more and more obstacles in front of you, then you should do some internal housecleaning and see what's going on: Do you hold the belief that you do not deserve to succeed? Do you have an inner conflict in relation to your goal? **If you feel that reality opposes you, it may be a reflection of your internal resistance.**

For example, Sharon was a graphic designer who joined one of my workshops a few months after she had given birth to her first child. Sharon tried to return to the world of graphic design, but was repeatedly turned down by all the employers she approached. She felt that she was entering a dead-end street. In one of the exercises in the workshop we examined the career-related patterns of Sharon's family members. Sharon realized that giving birth had triggered a family vs. career conflict that had been latently present in her family as she was growing up. Sharon's father was a talented and accomplished man who succeeded in many professional fields, but he was also an absent father who was not involved in the lives of his children. On the other hand, Sharon's mother devoted herself to her family, paying a personal price in giving up a career of her own. Give the absence of a role model at home, Sharon hadn't learned how to combine family and career, and felt she had to choose between the two. Searching for a job after the birth of her firstborn gave rise to the career-family conflict. She believed that pursuing a meaningful career would make her a negligent mother.

During the exercise, when Sharon faced the roots of her conflict, she chose another path and made a commitment to finding a way to combine both worlds in her life. What is interesting is that shortly after Sharon untied her inner knot, she felt the job search was going more smoothly. She was invited to more interviews and eventually found a job in the field of graphic design.

Maybe you are feeling resistance to my suggestion that an inner conflict is holding you back. You may say to yourself, "But I really want to achieve my goal. I really want to find a job/recruit clients/attract investors!"

Of course you do.

However, I am quite convinced that another voice within you opposes achieving your goal, probably out of fear. The inner conflict might manifest itself in becoming stuck, suffering repeated rejections and a feeling you're in a never-ending struggle. Reality is a mirror that reflects your inner ambivalence.

EXERCISE:
Identifying and overcoming barriers to success

The following exercise consists of two parts:

Day 1:

Ask yourself honestly: Why don't I want to reach my career goal? What can I lose if I achieve my career goal?

Or, write this title at the top of a page:
15 bad things that will happen if I achieve my career goal.

Write down all the answers that come to mind, even if something seems silly at the moment. Do not judge any answer that pops up. Every answer is welcome because it gives you a real chance to identify the barriers that lie underneath the surface of your professional life.

Day 2:

Read the list of answers you wrote on the first day.

1. *Ask yourself about each answer: Is this really the **absolute truth?** If it is the truth – is it really that bad? Do I know any exceptions? What can I do about it?*

2. *Consider the inverse of each answer and open your mind to it. Try to make the inverse sentences a commitment to yourself.*

For example: Say you wrote, "If I achieve my career goal I will have to work late every day." Ask yourself: Is that the absolute truth? If it is the truth – is it that bad? Do you know people who succeed and yet work reasonable hours? What can you do about it so that you succeed and still have free time on your hands?

Look at the inverse of the sentence: "If I achieve my career goal I will have more free time." Think about it. Is it possible? Open up your mind to the possibility, and see if any new ideas emerge in the next few days.

Incidentally, a common barrier to success is an inner resistance to making money. I recommend doing the above exercise with the following title: **15 bad things that will happen to me if I earn three times as much as I do now.**

The most painful barrier of all: feeling alone and helpless

Now, let's further tackle our barriers.

We all have moments of falling, disappointment and frustration. But do you feel it is more than that? Deep down, do you feel helpless? Alone? Does despair strike you at moments of weakness, but you suppress it, push it aside and try with all your power to look forward, think positive and keep on building your career? Sometimes positive thinking and self-reinforcement alone are not sufficient. If your inner experience is of loneliness and helplessness, then you should pay attention to it.

To illustrate this, imagine you're building a house on the beach. You are diligent and hard-working, you are using the best materials, erecting brick walls and investing in the best furnishings – and yet – the house is unstable. That's because it is built on shaky ground. In this case, it is not enough to focus on the construction, because if the foundation is shaky, the house will not hold up.

If you work hard to build your career, and you feel that it's too difficult a struggle and that you are not moving forward, it might be because your emotional and spiritual foundations are fragile. You feel insecure, alone and even without hope. It is very important and courageous to look inside and identify your mental infrastructure. Hand on heart, how much do you really believe in your ability to make a change, to have an impact and to build a stable, lasting and significant career?

Believing that you are worthy of success, that you are capable of making a difference, and that reality is basically in your favor are the emotional and spiritual foundations for building a long-term and prosperous career.

Many people, and perhaps you, too, have learned during their lives that their control over reality is quite limited. This realization may have come about as the result of a traumatic event in which you experienced an intense feeling of helplessness that was seared deep into your body and soul. Sometimes it's a cumulative effect of repeated failures in life's formative childhood years, like, for example, a dyslectic child who suffers recurring failures at school. In any case, the result is what is known in psychology as "learned helplessness," a mental state created by intense or multiple experiences of inability to affect the outcome of a situation. This, in turn, produces chronic feelings of despair and helplessness, and creates a pattern of passive behavior or ineffective action. It's a difficult feeling that sometimes leads to real depression.

Other feelings that you might have acquired through life experience are those of loneliness and distrust. You feel you can't rely on the help of others, but can only rely on yourself. You feel alone, even abandoned, and in a constant struggle to carve out your place and receive recognition. You feel you're the only one that can make things happen and that everything depends on you. This feeling may manifest itself in an obsessive need for control. Many people who suffer from loneliness and mistrust have an urge to control their own and their loved ones' affairs. They feel accountable even to events that are outside their control, and they are always anxious that things will fall apart if they do not take over.

Loneliness and distrust are feelings that quite a few people harbor. They are usually the result of intense or recurring childhood experiences that embed in you a belief that there is no one to trust, or that if you trusted others, you would get hurt. Hence, you can only rely on yourself. Belief of this kind, which was probably a survival mechanism in childhood, becomes an obstacle in adulthood, when we become control freaks and find it difficult to delegate responsibility or ask for help. Deep within ourselves we feel we are in a constant battle with reality. We are cautious and worried, and feel we must constantly be on guard. As a result, we block the emergence of our own huge potential and prevent our careers from blossoming.

I know these emotions well. In one of the sessions of a self-development course I attended, we worked on the fears that stop us from moving forward. One of the exercises was to pull a random card with a message on it from a deck, with the intention of learning something about our fear. The card I pulled said: "I need my environment in order to develop." For me, it was a most terrifying message. The idea of being dependent upon my surroundings was so intimidating because, being a child and entirely dependent on others, I experienced my environment as volatile, instable and not to be trusted. I lived in what one of my teachers called a "solo prison," having the feeling that I'd be better off relying only on myself, and finding it difficult to trust others in personal, and, later in life, professional aspects of my life.

Interdependence

My spiritual mentor introduced me to the concept of "interrelatedness" or "interdependence," which is a fundamental principle in many spiritual teachings, including Buddhism and Jewish Kabbalah. Interdependence is a phenomenon that exists in both physical and spiritual realms. For example, think about this very moment when you are reading these lines, and reflect on the countless conditions that were met for this moment to happen: the device you're reading from was manufactured in one country, the raw materials came from other geographic areas, and well-oiled systems of transportation and sales ensured that the device finally reached your desk. All these processes involve, of course, many people. And that's just a small segment of the necessary conditions. Perhaps a friend drew your attention to this book. I dedicated much time and energy to writing it, and it's based on the knowledge and experience of other people as well as myself. You get the point, right?

Interdependence also exists in less tangible realms. Not long ago I read in a blog of a family physician named Dr. Cicurel that in recent years a body of knowledge has been accumulating concerning our social relationships and their impact on our health. For example, when we do regular physical exercise, the odds increase that our acquaintances will also exercise regularly. When people around us are happy, it is more probable that we ourselves will be satisfied. What's interesting is that those interactive influences are not only found in direct connections. Individuals at far ends of the social spectrum and in diverse networks and communities – who do not even know each other – are mutually affected. It turns out that people influence each other in mysterious ways through social connections, and that human communities function somewhat like a school of fish – as one unit.

Jewish tradition has a saying: "In the way a man wants to go – on that path he will be led." That is, forces bigger than we are help us to move forward in the direction we want to go. Personally, I've seen many such cases: coincidences, unexpected phone calls and surprising encounters that occur just at the right moment. Here is an example of a relatively small incident: In my workshops I often use magazines to create collages. A few weeks ago I wondered how I'd get some high-quality magazines for a workshop that was going to take place soon. The next day an unfamiliar woman walked straight into my office and asked me if I needed some magazines, because her car's trunk was full of printed material she wanted to give away.

Einstein said: "We can't solve problems by using the same kind of thinking we used when we created them." If you believe you are the only one who controls your destiny, if you feel a need to constantly be in control, and if you have difficulty trusting others, then there needs to be a complete change, a 180-degree turnaround. Instead of looking for the solutions inside yourself, let go and trust life. Instead of taking responsibility for situations and conditions outside your control, learn to trust others as well.

You may be accustomed to trusting only yourself on many levels, even a spiritual one. You might believe in the Law of Attraction as introduced in the book and film *The Secret*. The Law of Attraction represents the belief that "like attracts like," so that by focusing on positive or negative thoughts, you can bring about positive or negative results. The Law of Attraction states that your thoughts create your own reality and therefore you are fully responsible for changing your life.

The notion of interdependence might sound incompatible with the Law of Attraction, and you may even feel resistance to it, as if it strips you of your own power. You may continue to feel that the only way your life will take a different turn is if you change yourself. Well, in this case you have turned the Law of Attraction into another locked door in your own solo prison, because you believe that everything is entirely up to you or to be controlled by your own thoughts and beliefs. (Personally, I believe that the extreme individualism of Western society, as embodied in the belief and value that anyone is solely responsible for their fate, is the root of a lot of misery, loneliness and alienation.)

In fact, interdependence does not contradict the perception that your beliefs create your reality. It only extends this principle, adds elasticity to it, and changes its focus a little. Accepting our interrelated existence expands our belief system to include the belief in the unknown and the infinite. It allows us to let go and open ourselves to guidance from forces of love that support our existence. These forces are larger than us, but not separate, because the power of love exists within us. We open ourselves to the support of reality even in dark places – when we are afraid, cannot see and do not know where to go from here. It's a bit like a baby's basic experience, protected in his mother's arms. Many of us haven't known this primal security, so accepting interdependence also means restoring our vulnerability, trusting that we are not alone, and knowing that help and guidance are available and that not everything depends on us.

Believing in interdependence does, in fact, create our reality. Our confidence in life opens up new possibilities that we've not yet even dreamed of.

This is also how we become open to abundance.

EXERCISE:
Being a part of the whole

If you feel helpless or alone, or that everything depends solely on you, I recommend you reconnect to interdependence. Restore your trust in other people and in life.
Open up to abundance.

My spiritual mentor gave me the following sentence to repeat and reflect on.

I offer it here for you:

"I trust the loving infinite power (or: light) to teach me, guide me and pull me out of this solo place and to connect me to interdependence."

It could be that this sentence generates resistance. Find out what that stems from. Is it resistance to the very notion of interdependence? Is it fear of losing control? To succeed in life and business, it is essential to be able to trust, and, to some degree, release control.

You are perfect exactly as you are

Along the path of building my career I discovered that one of the most deeply-rooted barriers that hindered me from moving forward was the fear of losing. I felt that losses I'd experienced in the past had hurt me so deeply that I preferred to fail and avoid success. This way I wouldn't lose what I had already achieved and get hurt again. I believed that success is crisis-prone, so I was afraid of it. Bottom line, I felt stuck; the desire to succeed was strong but so was the fear of succeeding.

In my distress, I turned to my spiritual mentor. "Your outlook on the world is dual," he said. To clarify, "dualism" is a perception that the world consists of contrasting elements – good vs. bad, success vs. failure and so on. Every experience is either on the positive pole (success/good) or the negative pole (failure/bad). Adopting the dualistic concept turns life into a constant struggle to hold on to the positive pole and eradicate or escape from the negative one. In the context of career, life is a continuous effort to succeed and escape failure.

My mentor talked further about **the concept of "non-duality" – a notion of perfection or wholeness where there is nothing to fix, change or achieve.** We are whole just as we are. There is nothing to hold on to and nothing to escape from. Perfection exists in a dimension where there is no duality, so there is no option of failure. Similarly, the Buddha talked about our human nature as a clean spotless curtain. All emotions, mental fluctuations and experiences are just spots on the curtain. They do not in any way affect our inner nature, which is complete in and of itself. The practice of meditation considers the changing states of consciousness as an exterior layer to our essence, which is complete, peaceful and enlightened. Meditation is not a way to "fix" us, but to remind us of who we really are.

My mentor guided me to trust my wholeness, where no correction at all is needed, the place (soul, if you wish) that is like a clean white curtain impervious to failure or damage.

Although I was already familiar with this idea on an intellectual level, it was difficult to emotionally internalize it. Maybe you feel the same way, because it has been engrained in us to relate to the world in a dualistic way. Most of us feel "broken" in some places and so engage in changing our thinking and amending our personalities. We also identify breakdowns in the world around us and we work on repairing them and "collecting the broken pieces." Mental or spiritual processes are often perceived as "moving forward" or "repairing" a previous existence which had been broken or spoiled. But a mended plate can always break again. This is the tragedy of this perspective. So we should always be on guard not to fall or break down again.

Believing in my wholeness has been one of the main keys to my liberation from fear of failing and getting hurt again. It also liberated me from having to labor at changing my beliefs and perceptions. Because our perfection is our true nature.

Getting back to this truth is like turning on a light which all at once illuminates every dark corner.

Failure, like other life crises, could be a turning point in changing your mindset. If you have experienced a painful failure, or a sequence of repeated failures, it could be that you'll need to develop completely new conceptual tools to deal with the situation.

A shift to the perceptions presented here – believing in interdependence and in non-duality – are examples of my learning process in the face of failures. I recommend being open to new ideas in the process of building your career.

They might change you and affect other areas of your life far beyond the professional aspect.

EXERCISE:
Connecting to your wholeness

If you find it difficult to connect to your wholeness, to the place that cannot be broken no matter what you go through or what happens to you, my recommendation is to simply ask to open up to it.

Try to trust your wholeness, even if you have no idea what it feels like and where it might take you. Ask for guidance and wait. When the answer comes – you will know.

It is also the place where miracles can originate.

Further insights into and tips regarding failure and disappointment

Remember: no matter how successful you are, you will always fail again: Mike, one of my group-facilitation teachers, told me something I will never forget: a good workshop is one where 70% of the participants are satisfied with it and 30% are not. If everyone is happy with the workshop it's probably not really good; it's middle-of-the-road and not terribly challenging. I try to apply this rule in other facets of my business and personal life as well. If your work is valuable, then being successful means you fail at least thirty percent of the time with thirty percent of the people.

Michael Jordan said:

> *I've missed more than 9,000 shots in my career. I've lost almost 300 games. Twenty-six times I've been trusted to take the game-winning shot and I missed. I've failed over and over and over again in my life. And that is why I succeed.*

Failure is essential: it's your guide to making wiser decisions in the future. The more mistakes you make, the more focused and experienced you get, and you gain a better understanding of your business. I once read an article that maintained that the richest people in the world went bankrupt at least twice. So if you fail – you're in good company! Having the courage to fail and taking away new lessons from failures are critical practices in becoming truly successful.

This reminds me of an interesting and quite surprising bit of research I've read about quitting smoking cigarettes. It said that the overall percentage of people who quit smoking is small, but the chances of quitting for good are higher among those who tried to quit (but relapsed) several times. That is, the chances of quitting smoking are higher among those who try and fail – and then try again – than among those who never try.

It's always darkest before dawn: The darkest and most despairing moments are often the low point from which new growth begins. Although it can be very tempting to cease trying, do keep in mind that many people report they had experienced great despair and a strong desire to give up just a moment before they made their breakthrough. Similarly, writer Napoleon Hill noticed: "Most great people have attained their greatest success just one step beyond their greatest failure." My friend Anna calls it "the 101 treatment". She and her husband went through difficult, expensive and unsuccessful fertility treatments, only to despair and stop trying. But a moment before giving up they decided to give the treatment one final chance, from which Anna became pregnant.

The Law of Large Numbers: Sales statistics indicate that most clients will say "No" to the sale, and a minority will say "Yes." This principle also applies to job interviews, launching events, internet sales and so on. Most prospective customers will decline your offer, and a relatively small percent will accept it. Hence, every "No" brings you closer to a "Yes." Sales and marketing professionals know that, so they develop a thick skin towards negative client responses.

Adam, one of the best salespeople I ever knew, was a car insurance agent in a large company. One of the features that distinguished him from the rest of the agents was that he didn't hesitate to offer customers all kinds of policies even when he knew that his prices were significantly higher than the competition's. Other agents didn't do it because they assumed that there was no point in trying to sell costly policies. "Most people say 'No' to me," admitted Adam, "but then along comes the tenth client and they make a deal with me." Adam didn't give in to one of the most common fears: fear of rejection. He was willing to hear "No" and not let it hold him back. Those expensive policies that he sold had set him apart from the other agents. His name always appeared on the list of the outstanding agents who received the highest bonuses.

The Law of Large Numbers gives me, as I hope it will give you too, the strength to turn to the customer who will probably turn you down, to contact the HR department who rejected you in the past, or flirt with that person who looks totally out of your league. Perhaps the odds are against you, and you might be afraid of rejection, but statistics show that a certain percentage will say that "Yes" you so want to hear.

Have realistic expectations: One definition of failure is the gap between expectations and their realization; if expectations are unrealistic then failure is inevitable. An example of this is Sharona, a medical cosmetician who opened a new clinic in her neighborhood and organized a beautiful launch event promoting treatments at half price. Much to her disappointment, only two new clients booked treatments. She said: "I'm desperate. If only two clients responded to my special offer maybe I have no possibility of success." I said to Sharona that if she expected dozens of new clients after her first launch evening, then it's only natural that she feels despair. Sharona understood she's got a long road ahead of her, and scaled back her expectations for immediate success. She organized another event where two more customers bought treatments. This time Sharona defined the evening as a success.

It's all in eye of the beholder: What you perceive as failure might be great success in the eyes of your customers. One of the most touching examples is the story of Nicky, a good friend who works as a therapist with at-risk youth. Nicky told me about a boy who came to therapy over a period of time and sat in silence during their meetings, despite Nicky's attempts to get him to talk. Sometimes the boy would throw out a laconic reply like "Everything's all right," or "Things are so-so," and that would be it. Things went on like this for a whole year, and Nicky felt he had failed as a therapist. "I felt like a failure," he said. "If the boy hadn't persisted and come every week I would have suggested that welfare authorities refer him to a different therapist." At the end of the year, in the very last session, the boy said to Nicky in his curt way: "Thank you for listening to me ..." Underneath his silent demeanor he was experiencing the treatment as a space of listening and understanding. The treatment which Nicky saw as a failure comprised apparently valuable sessions for the boy.

My advice is to ask for feedback from the people around you before you define something as a failure. You might be surprised to find that some people think highly of you and your work.

Correcting an error can increase your value even more: A study in a restaurant examined the impact of complaint-handling on customer satisfaction. The first test group received a delicious juicy steak, while the second group received a dry burnt one. The subjects from the second group who complained about their dry steak were then served the same delicious juicy steak that the first group received to begin with. Assessment of the satisfaction level of the two test groups revealed that subjects of the second group – whose complaints were handled – were more satisfied with the service than the first group.

That is, if you take responsibility for your mistakes and rectify whatever you can, your value will rise in the eyes of your customers. You may sometimes even appear more valuable than had you not made the mistake at all. When you do make mistakes, those who work with you will distinguish between the specific errors and your true qualities if you are transparent and open and run a thorough investigation. Your clients or employers will learn that they can rely on you. There cannot be substituted for anything.

Avoid rushed decision-making: If you make a mistake or fail, do not act immediately. Process the case in depth, think quietly and only then decide on a course of action. In an interview with Olympic judoka Arik Zeevi, he refers to his failure at the Beijing Olympics as what he calls "a colossal failure."

> *One thing is very important at the very first moment of failure when all you want to do is throw away the garment and say you quit … One of the most important things to understand is not to make decisions in the first moments of failure, that point when any decision we make only reflects emotions and is not necessarily the right decision. That's why I said to myself: "Wait a month or two after Beijing, and if it's still burning inside you, then you can quit." I'm happy that I didn't make a decision to retire, because after a week or two I decided I wanted to continue and I went on to four magical years marked by many successes.*

The successes include a gold medal at the 2012 European Championships, making Zeevi the oldest athlete to ever win a gold medal at that competition.

When you do fail, it's sometimes more constructive to take a break, step back or go on vacation. Take time to "lick your wounds" and process your emotions, feelings and thoughts before you make a practical decision regarding the future.

Prevent crises: There is a saying: "You can't make the same mistake twice. The second time you make it, it's no longer a mistake, it's a choice." In some cases this is true. One of the best ways to deal with crises is to avert them, especially when they are predictable. For example, many therapists suffer a decline in income during the holiday season, whereas this is a peak sales period in commerce. If you look at the expected annual revenue of your business, you won't be surprised over and over again (as many are) by a revenue decrease in the low season, and you'll be prepared and available to provide service during the peak seasons.

Prepare ahead for a potential failure: Emotionally, this is perhaps one of the most difficult tips to act upon when you aim for success. Still, risk assessment must take into account the possibility that the worst will happen, and you must be prepared for it. You should always have more goals and backup plans. Ignoring the plausibility of failure is a natural and understandable coping strategy, but it can be devastating.

This is one of the conclusions of a young man named Nir Schneider, whose childhood dream (from the age of three) was to become an air force pilot in the Israel Defense Forces (IDF). The air force training course is one of the toughest and most prestigious courses in the IDF, and of the very few that are accepted to it, many are expelled during the course. One of those expelled was Schneider. He relates in a touching and sincere post on his blog about how his dream shattered to pieces and he was left depressed, lost, and wallowing in self-pity. He says he had never considered other options, which made his failure that much more devastating. He recommends that all aspirants set alternative goals in case their first choice doesn't materialize.

Failure as a crisis: A failure can be extremely painful. In some cases it feels like the world ends and nothing else is of value. The shattering of a dream can involve symptoms of severe loss and life-crisis. In such cases, mourning is a normal and natural reaction. Sometimes it is necessary to mourn over unfulfilled expectations, over days and hours invested "in vain," and over life that took a sharp turn. In such cases, as with any other kinds of loss, you will usually go through an initial period of grief and pain-processing, and after that you will recover your passion again and set new goals.

Failure, like any other crisis, can also be a lever for growth. It might be a real opportunity to do some soul searching and re-calibrate before setting off again. In my twenties I dreamed of becoming a singer, and decided to pursue my dream and learn to sing professionally. After two years of studying it finally dawned on me: I was nothing more than a mediocre vocalist. My disappointment left me bitter at first, but then I realized that my need to sing stemmed from a deeper passion – to touch others and express my unique voice. I then found my calling through the two channels of writing and working with people.

Support: A supportive environment can be a lifesaver in times of crisis. Encouragement, trust, and emotional and economic support could be your fulcrum in those moments when you lose faith in yourself. Nir Schneider, the ousted pilot whose story I told earlier says:

> *I was lucky there was someone who cared for me and encouraged me and believed in me when I had given up on myself ... I owe everything to that good friend who returned the smile to my face. Thanks to him, I'm on my feet again right now, and very soon I will walk and even run, and someday I'll fly like I would have flown before.*

Naftali Bennett, the politician and hi-tech entrepreneur, described in an interview to the newspaper *Makor Rishon* how an unexpected source of support enabled his company to launch their successful product which was later sold for millions of dollars. The source was the grandmother of one of the partners. Bennett relates:

> *After we invested two years in a product that totally failed in the market, we had some initial success with the new product. We went to the company's investors and asked for another chance. They agreed to give us only $2.5 million of the $3.5 million that were needed, and demanded that we find the extra million elsewhere. On the due date we had 3.3 million and assumed they would cut us some slack and contribute the rest, but they said: 'No, if you do not raise $200,000 by tonight, we are closing the company.' Eventually, the grandmother of one of our group members took all her savings and invested $200,000 in the company. From that moment on, our goal was to return Grandma's money to her, with interest. Finally we gave her $600,000 dollars.*

Remember the interrelatedness between you and your environment. Success and optimism in your close environment will raise your energy levels as well. Surround yourself with positive, successful and energetic people. Deliberately look for them and stick with them. A positive attitude is contagious. In my case one of the most supportive and inspiring people in my life is my relative Roger, a dear man who is ninety-four years of age. Take the example of his second marriage in his seventies (!) after the death of his first wife, as an indication of his incredible life energy and positive outlook. Despite his advanced age, Roger is one of the most dynamic, optimistic and young-at-heart people I know. Every time we talk he says to me: "I believe in you. I'm sure you'll succeed. If you work hard and don't give up you will achieve everything you want." Roger is a constant reminder to me that mental age is not dependent on physical age and is much more important than a chronological count. One can find meaning in life at any age.

You can draw inspiration from biographies and films about successful people, and from videos and online lectures on sites like YouTube and TED. Life stories of successful people will remind you that all successful people had to deal with setbacks, resistance and crises along the way.

Self-punishment or forgiveness: Buddha said that in every crisis people can choose whether to pierce themselves with one arrow or two. The first arrow is the crisis itself, the objective difficulty of the circumstances, while the second arrow is the pain, criticism and self-blame people inflict on themselves, thus causing additional suffering. A failure, mistake or crisis can cause damage, but the greater suffering usually stems from the emotional and subjective meaning we attach to it. Failure becomes an issue if you see it as a sign of weakness. Failure is painful if you associate it with shame, guilt and punishment. Failure can be devastating if you give it a future meaning that affects your chances of moving forward. If you have failed, forgive yourself. Do not burden yourself with more suffering.

Half a measure is no measure: At what point do you determine whether you succeeded or failed? After how many attempts do you stop trying? Are you able to distinguish between the big picture and the specific errors along the way? Napoleon Hill figured about a century ago that "one of the most common causes for failure is the habit of quitting when one is overtaken by temporary defeat." Thomas A. Edison, one of the most prolific inventors in history (there is a record 1093 patents in his name), was also a very persistent and determined man. He is known for saying: "I have not failed. I've just found 10,000 ways that won't work."

An example of someone looking at the overall picture is Moses, my relative who realized his dream to open a restaurant. He closed the restaurant after two years of financial difficulties. However, optimistic and determined as always, Moses decided to open a new business in the field of natural medicine. Although some of those around him thought the restaurant was a passing episode of failure, Moses perceived it as a stepping stone in his learning and development as a businessman. The experience and knowledge he gained in the marketing, managerial and financial aspects of running a business also helped him later in the field of natural medicine.

Find goals you love: One of the best tips to help deal with failure is to ask yourself: "What do I really like to do?" Sometimes failure is the stimulus that triggers you to ask all the right questions about your choices, your motives and what is important to you. Failure can help you to choose the next goal that reignites the flames of passion.

The singer Jewel writes on the cover of her album *Pieces of You* that she thanks all the bosses who fired her, thus forcing her to do the one thing she's really good at – singing.

In his Stanford speech, Steve Jobs spoke about the crisis he'd experienced when he was fired from Apple at the age of 30, and what helped him overcome it:

> *I was a very public failure, and I even thought about running away from the valley. But something slowly began to dawn on me – I still loved what I did. The turn of events at Apple had not changed that one bit. I had been rejected, but I was still in love.*

And so I decided to start over. I didn't see it then, but it turned out that getting fired from Apple was the best thing that could have ever happened to me. The heaviness of being successful was replaced by the lightness of being a beginner again, less sure about everything. It freed me to enter one of the most creative periods of my life.

During the next five years, I started a company named NeXT, another company named Pixar, and fell in love with an amazing woman who would become my wife ... I'm pretty sure none of this would have happened if I hadn't been fired from Apple. It was an awful tasting medicine, but I guess the patient needed it. Sometimes life hits you in the head with a brick. Don't lose faith. **I'm convinced that the only thing that kept me going was that I loved what I did.** *You've got to find what you love. And that is as true for your work as it is for your lovers.*

Remind yourself of your initial motivation: Failure or crisis can make it crystal-clear to you that you really love what you do. You ask yourself: "Why did I embark on this adventure?" and discover that you did it for all the right reasons. You realize that your heart, your passion and your motivation are entrenched in the career you have chosen. In such case, failure is an opportunity to remember your initial motivation. The more you are at peace with your choice, the less you will be bothered by the obstacles along the way, and the failures you will experience won't despair you.

Think about a failure as a teaspoon of salt; if you put a teaspoon of salt in a glass of water it will surely become salty. On the other hand, if you put a teaspoon of salt in a pool of water it won't have any impact whatsoever. This is how your motivation works. The more you understand your choice, identify with it, and know that it comes from the depths of your being, the less you will be affected by those unpleasant life events that we call failures.

THANK YOU FOR PURCHASING THIS BOOK!

Your opinion means a lot to me.
Please write a review on the book's page on Amazon.com
to let me know your thoughts.

WANT MORE?
Download a special FREE bonus:

10 Hot Tips to Finding Your Career Path
without Losing Your Mind

Link to download the Free bonus:
http://activepage.co.il/TenHotTips

For more insights and tips
come and visit me on my Facebook page:
https://www.facebook.com/FisherMichal